Life Clues

Unlocking the Lessons to an Exceptional Life

ANGELA C. SANTOMERO

◄ BOOKS & MEDIA ►

CHICAGO

Cover art credits
Front: Aleksandra Konoplia/Moment/Getty Images, Katsumi
Murouchi/Moment/Getty Images, Arunna/Shutterstock

Back: Image of Daniel Tiger: Provided under license from
Fred Rogers Productions.

Nickelodeon's *Blue's Clues* used with permission.
© 2023 Viacom International Inc.
All Rights Reserved.

Author Photo: Courtesy of the Author, Angela C. Santomero

ISBN: 978-0-8294-5634-9
Library of Congress Control Number: 2023944243

Printed in the United States of America.
23 24 25 26 27 28 29 30 31 32 Versa 10 9 8 7 6 5 4 3 2 1

Table of Contents

A Few Words from Steve

Hi, it's me, Steve Burns. I was the original host of *Blue's Clues*.

The one with the green stripes. . . yeah, that one.

Okay, so do you want to hear something weird and cool?

You do? Great!

So, a zillion years ago when I had hair, I moved to New York to be a gritty theater actor. I never thought about being on children's TV, but then I went to this strange audition and BOOM—I found myself wearing green stripes, talking to condiments, and finding clues as an accidental educator to an entire generation of children. Whoa!

A zillion years later, here's what still surprises me: I'm now an enthusiastic grown-up student of many of the same lessons I was tasked to impart to children, which you will find in this nifty book by my friend

Angela C. Santomero. Talking to kids every day with the deepest respect for their curious "beginner's minds" has allowed me to cultivate a sense of wonder that helps me see beauty in the ordinary, problems as opportunities, and challenges as clues on a journey toward greater understanding.

Cool, right?

You look great by the way.

Steve

All of us, at some time or other, need help. Whether we're giving or receiving help, each one of us has something valuable to bring to this world. That's one of the things that connects us as neighbors—in our own way, each one of us is a giver and a receiver.

—FRED ROGERS

I'm so glad you're here!

—XO Angela

A Note for You

Dear Reader,

I have always paid close attention to the little "clues" that life has shown me. These clues, or glimmers of clarity in the chaos of life, helped me pay attention to what mattered most and helped me find my life's passion and purpose. I wholeheartedly believe that everyone has their own life clues, and with a little coaching you can learn to pay attention to what matters most. Not to spoil the ending, but tapping into your own life clues will add more fulfillment, more passion, and more purpose to your own life—and that's why I wrote this book.

For me, clues pop up where I least expect them. Years before *Super Why!*, *Blue's Clues,* and *Daniel Tiger's Neighborhood* existed as thoughts in my mind, I was attending a meeting in the research department at Nickelodeon in New York City. Wide-eyed, eager, and fresh out of college, I was "in the room where it happened" ("it" being the magic of creating TV shows). As a child, I had been a huge fan of *Mister*

Rogers' Neighborhood. As a young person, I dreamed of one day working in the glamorous world of TV and doing what Fred Rogers did: create TV shows that talked to rather than down to kids.

Well, here I was, a newbie in my twenties, sitting with some of the most inventive and creative people in the world of television programming. I felt honored to be included in a meeting where decisions were made about which children's shows would air on TV. I listened intently as each department weighed in on what was important to them and how they would be impacted by the big decisions that were about to be made. As participants interrupted or spoke over one another, I sat quietly and observed.

Suddenly, the head of the preschool television department turned to me and asked, "Well, what do you think we should do for preschoolers, Angela?"

Even though I had been paying attention to everything that was being said, I instinctively sat up taller. I felt my heart begin to race. For a moment my mind went blank, and then I remember thinking that this was one of those times in life that felt like jumping off the high dive. Sink or swim. And so, after pausing for a second, I took a deep breath and spoke from the heart.

I don't recall the exact words, but I do remember that everyone had been focused on the business—the costs, timing, talent, and direction—of television. But I spoke about kids—real kids, the kind whose family is their world, whose eyes light up with new information, and whose work is play.

At that time, I was one of only a few people at Nickelodeon who had worked directly with young children. I didn't stand on a soapbox, but I did speak from the heart about who preschoolers are, what they need, what makes them laugh, and what kind of TV show I thought they would love. I talked about the impact Mister Rogers had made on me when I was a child and how the goal of a show should be to make kids feel seen and heard.

And then, silence. I mean, *crickets*.

Let me tell you, those few seconds of silence were nerve-racking. I played it cool on the outside, but on the inside, I was panicking. *Did I say too much? Did I go too far? Do I still have a job?* In fact, I had already jumped. Sink or swim, I had to finish the dive. I took another deep breath, prayed I wouldn't belly flop, and talked about how I could be an advocate for kids at a television network dedicated to making TV shows expressly for them.

To my surprise, the energy in the room shifted. People started talking about kids and brainstorming child-focused ideas.

That moment when I felt like I was on the highest high dive? Turns out I didn't smack the water spread-eagled. Maybe it wasn't the cleanest dive in the world, but I think if it were the Olympics, the Russian judges would have given me an 8.7. In any case, once I hit the water, I swam.

In routinely diving into the unknown in my professional and personal life, I learned several lessons, but this one stands out: Life gives us signs. Life offers clues about how we can find success, fulfillment, and joy. It's up to us to pay attention and follow them.

On that particular day oh, so many years ago, I realized that I had found my life's purpose, which is to be an advocate for children in a business run by adults. In essence, my purpose was to change the lives of children and adults for the better.

I was invited to attend more high-powered meetings and weigh in on other important decisions. With each brainstorming session and every decision, I knew that I was inching toward my goal of honoring Fred Rogers in my own way (more on that later). I reached this goal by writing and creating first *Blue's Clues* and then *Daniel Tiger's Neighborhood.*

But that process of listening, observing, sharing, and standing firm in my convictions gave me more than professional achievement. This wasn't only about having a seat in the room, or, eventually, a place of privilege at the head of the conference table. Those meetings showed me that success and happiness are within reach if we pay attention to the children. And why not? Kids can be our greatest teachers; it is from them that we can learn the most important lessons in life.

In the days, weeks, months, and years that followed that meeting, I started paying attention to the clues that life gives us, especially those clues that come from kids. For me it's become a daily habit to notice the small things that say a lot. For instance, years ago, when I would read fairy tales to my nephew, he would ask questions like: "Why is the big bad wolf so big and bad? Why is Little Red Riding Hood walking all alone in the woods?" Those were great questions that helped inspire the development of my show *Super Why!* I also started hearing kids singing everywhere around me—in the supermarket checkout line, "Waiting, it's so hard to wait on a line!" or when a child would sing to his dad at the beach, "Some days we're at the beach, some days we're at the pool, but it doesn't matter, I just wanna be with you!" These were little gems and I stored them away in my brain for future use. I also started seeing the book *The Artist's Way: A Spiritual Path to Higher Creativity* by Julia Cameron. I figured this was a sign that I should read it. When I finally did, the philosophy spoke to me, and I started creative writing for the first time. These clues helped me tap into my true self, which in turn enabled me to fulfill my own purpose in life. I firmly believe that these clues can help you fulfill your purpose, too.

I've learned a lot of things over the years, but my greatest teachers have been children. When we pay attention to the small and the big things kids do, we change not only ourselves; we change the world.

With love,
Angela

P.S. Keep an eye out for some **bolded** clues throughout the book. When you piece them together, they unveil a message to be shared with everyone.

I Like You Just the Way You Are

It's you I like. Every part of you—
Your skin, your eyes, your feelings
whether old or new.
I hope that you'll remember
even when you're feeling blue
that it's you I like.

—FRED ROGERS

It happened when I was watching TV.

I was four years old and sitting on the floor in my living room and staring at the screen. Mister Rogers started singing "It's You I Like." I now know that he was singing to tens of thousands of children that day, but when I was four it felt like he was singing just to me. And those words were exactly what I needed to hear.

At a young age, I fell into the trap of needing to be perfect in how I looked, what I said, and how I behaved. Yes, it started when I was around four years old. Like most children, I wanted to please my parents, but the rules seemed to change daily, and I could never live up to their expectations. Looking back, I see that my parents' definition of perfect was what they wanted me to be at any given time. Be fun when they were in a good mood. Be quiet when they weren't. And no matter what I did, I could have done it better. When I got life wrong, the consequences were painful. When I got it right, I felt invincible.

I started to chase the invincible feeling, wanting desperately to be liked just the way I was. But it was hard. As a child, I saw unfairness and truths in my family that no one else around me seemed to see or acknowledge. I said things out loud that no one wanted to hear. As I grew older and started to have my own opinions, feelings, and aspirations, the distance between my family and me grew. I was taught that negativity was armor. What do I mean by this? If I lowered my expectations, I could shield myself from pain. If I didn't love hard, I wouldn't be hurt. If I didn't dream, I would protect myself from failure.

As I lived my life with this fear-based mentality, a judgmental inner voice began to develop. I called it the Wicked Witch, and it nagged at me all the time: "You'll never be beautiful . . . You'll never be thin . . . You'll never get into college . . . You don't have any friends." This, of course, made me a rather moody, confused child.

One shining light in those early formative years was having someone positive around me. And by "around me," I mean via the television set. Mister Rogers' kindness held the Wicked Witch at bay. When Mister Rogers would tell everyone watching his show that "I like you just the way you are," I felt as if he was talking directly to me. I felt seen for who I was. I felt as if I was being given a warm hug—and let me tell you, I really needed to be hugged.

Those words—"I like you just the way you are"— planted a seed in my heart that took some time to grow. But grow, it did. Armed with a new point of view, thanks to the words of Fred Rogers, I started to find new sources of truth. Instead of hearing the voice of the Wicked Witch telling me, "You can't," I began to push back with, "I can." I read every happily-ever-after book I could get my hands on, just to fuel my dreams and cultivate my passions. As a teenager, I "skidooed" into every feel-good movie in an attempt to write a better ending to my own story. Like Tess McGill in *Working Girl*, I had a fire in my belly. Like Andy Dufresne in *The Shawshank Redemption*, I followed hope as I chiseled my way out of my upbringing. Books and movies offered **LIFE CLUES** about having a vision, persevering, and believing in myself. The

> **The more I trusted my gut and my heart, the more serendipity showed up in my life.**

more I trusted my gut and my heart, the more serendipity showed up in my life. It was as if the greater appreciation of myself created a glow that had the effect of attracting good people and exhilarating opportunities. I started to find my people—the people I was in sync with, the ones who appreciated me and my big ideas. You know: people who liked me just the way I was. And I liked them just the way they were, too!

It was from these confidence-building experiences that my life's purpose unfolded. My inspiration was

Mister Rogers. Like him, I wanted all children to grow up hearing that someone liked them just the way they are. When kids hear this message of affirmation and live with this attitude of acceptance, they grow into adults who see the good in themselves and others.

Sensei Paul Castagno, a fifth-degree black belt, has dedicated his life to helping people realize they are much stronger than they think through martial arts. He says, "Sometimes, during our lowest moments, all it takes is for someone to believe in us to help us find our own inner strength." More often than not, we never know the full power and reach of our own faith in and appreciation of other people. It is likely that these infusions into the world made a huge difference for someone, somewhere.

This is my goal. If you didn't hear it every day in your real life, I want you to hear it straight from me: I believe in you, and I like you just the way you are.

I believe in you, and I like you just the way you are.

JUST THE WAY WE ARE IN REAL LIFE

THE POWER OF A COMPLIMENT:

Even a comment as small as "I like your shoes!" can brighten someone's day. Never underestimate the far-reaching impact of kindness, interest, and an indication to someone that "You are seen."

THE POWER OF ADVOCACY:

Everyone needs an advocate. Be an advocate for everyone who populates your world—your child, your partner, your parents, grandparents, coworker, your dog. Remind them that you are there for them. In other words, make sure they know that you like them for who they are.

THE POWER OF MUSIC:

Music is therapeutic. It can change your mood almost instantaneously. When you need an extra boost, go to power ballads with strong, uplifting, hopeful lyrics that will immerse you in a world of positivity. As you listen to these songs, imagine you are in your own theme song, or your own music video, ready to conquer the world. (Some of my go-to songs are "Unstoppable" by Sia and Natasha Bedingfield's "Unwritten.")

LIFE CLUE #2

Take a Moment

Hi, out there! It's me.

Have you seen Blue, my puppy?

—BLUE'S CLUES

Before we jump into LIFE CLUE #2, let's first take a little moment . . .

Did you feel it? That moment of stillness in a few seconds of silence? Did you see the big white space between the first sentence of this chapter and these lines? Did you sense that something special happened?

With all the noise of the day, the clatter that surrounds us, and the chatter that happens inside us, the pause between thoughts is a brief moment of peace during which something else, something potentially ineffable, can happen.

Taking a small moment in time makes a big difference. I would go so far as to say that a well-timed pause changes everything. This small moment of space is the difference between listening, and hearing with the heart. It stirs our attention. It allows us to take a deep breath and focus our mind.

Looked at one way, a moment is nothing. It's a little hiccup in time. A beat of silence. It's the space between the notes in music, the space between words that **are** spoken. It's the space between one person's contribution and another person's response.

But looked at another way, a moment to breathe is *everything*. What exists within the small beats of silence is nothing less than magic. Magic! These are the gaps during which infinite possibilities involving courage, self-esteem, and respect can happen.

You know that feeling you get deep inside when someone *looks* at you? Like, really *sees* you? That flutter of hope you feel when you see genuine interest in their eyes? The surge of connection you feel when you see sincerity and concern? The feeling of validation that reassures you when you see compassion in someone's face?

When someone truly listens to you, you feel heard. You feel understood, and even if they might not really understand, you know that they *care*. This feeling is at the center of the programs I create for children.

Imagine you are sitting in front of the television. *Blue's Clues** is on. The blue puppy's human, a guy named Steve, draws you in by asking questions. He looks straight into the camera as he poses a question *to you*. Then he stops. He leans way in.

> **When someone truly listens to you, you feel heard.**

His eyes are twinkling, and you know why. He is interested in you, the viewer. He wants to know if you can help him. He wants to know where his puppy, Blue, is. In order to get kids to help him, he *knows* he needs to listen, so Steve stays there in those beats of silence for what seems like a long time. In other words, he takes a breath to let kids know that he cares what they think.

---

* *Blue's Clues* (and later *Blue's Clues and You*) is a children's television program that was first broadcast in 1996 and continues to be aired on PBS and NICK Jr. The show centers on a puppy named Blue and her friend (Steve, or Joe, or Josh, depending on the year the episode aired), who play a game to discover different clues. The show's detective-mystery and game format teaches children and adults about the powers of observation, critical thinking, kindness, and friendship.

It's in this gap moment between spoken words that the magic happens. You can even *feel* the magic. This is when the monologue becomes a dialogue. Since Steve is waiting for your answer, you talk to the screen.

Why?

Steve's pause indicates that your answer is important, that what you say matters.

And so, you share your thoughts.

In carving out a small breathing space from the onrush of the world, Steve has given you a chance to think, make a decision, and then answer the question.

Preschoolers understand that when people pause, they are being respectful. They are signaling that they are bringing all their attention to this moment. *Blue's Clues* scripts were written with two important concepts as the foundation of every episode: everyone needs to be heard, and everyone deserves to be listened to.

For our purposes here, we need to see this interaction between Steve and the viewer as the basis for the heart and soul of what we should expect in our own lives, too. It's not just the words that Steve says or the earnest way he says them. It's not only the hopeful intention or the warm tone of his voice. It's not precisely the look in his eyes as he waits for our answer. *It's all of it.* Steve is modeling a healthy give-and-take relation-ship, one based on making observations, being patient, showing respect, and being interested in the other person. Interest is the cornerstone of respectful rela-tionships. When we raise our children from babyhood with this kind of respectful attention to what is going on in their minds, they will grow up with enough self-worth to expect this high level of regard throughout their lives.

Many of us may not have grown up in a give-and-take environment, so we might have some catching up to do. We, too, need to be heard, understood, and val-ued. One way to cultivate these important characteris-tics is to get in the habit of taking a pause. This pause can happen during a conversation, when we pause to truly hear what the other person is saying. This pause can also happen after writing an angry email, because we can choose to reconsider and hit *delete* instead of *send.* We can pause throughout the day when we are busy or frustrated and, in the silence, give thanks. It's good to pause and remind ourselves that if we have enough money to buy gas or own an iPhone, then we are in a prosperous state. We are among the luckiest.

Taking a moment is *the* bedrock LIFE CLUE that helps create a magical state of being, because when we pause, we open up space. Take a breath. Be still. Don't speak. Try to harness your thoughts. Focus on your steady breathing and find within you a place of stillness. And then, if you are in a conversation with someone who has just finished saying something, ask a question. Each time we ask someone a question, we are extending an invitation to connect. Want to take your conversation even further? Try asking a vulnerable question. Asking a question can forge a connection; asking a *vulnerable* question deepens that bond ten times over.

When Steve asked if we had spotted a clue or identified the shape of a bunch of grapes (the shape's a triangle, FYI!), he was being vulnerable. Why is this being vulnerable? Because he admitted he didn't know the answer, and then asked for help. Try being vulnerable. Ask a question that shows you don't know everything and that you are curious and are interested to learn. It can be risky or awkward to ask someone a question. If you think about it, most of the time we don't know the answer. But even if we don't know the answer, we are demonstrating that we want to listen and understand. We are forging a deeper connection.

The length of the beat changes depending on the age of the person. Little ones need more time to think about the question, collect their thoughts, and then figure out how to verbalize what they're thinking. Sometimes this can take a long time, but trust me, it's worth the wait! Kids are brilliant, and their worldview is insightful and interesting. The same is true for adults. When we have time to think and no one is stuffing the beats of silence with chatter, we are more able to participate insightfully.

We wrote and directed *Blue's Clues* to have it feel as if Steve literally can't do anything until he has your response. *Blue's Clues* cannot continue without your help; everything stops until you participate. That's how important what you have to say is.

Following the pause, whether you talked to the TV or answered the question in your head, you saw Steve's whole expression light up. By continuing to make eye contact through the camera, he confirmed that he had heard you. For example, Steve may have asked, "Will you help me?" Then he pauses. It's a given rule in television programming that you're not supposed to have too much silence, which is known as "dead air." But *Blue's Clues* proved that kids have active and engaged minds, and when we give them time to respond, they experience a sense of joy. With a look of pure happiness on his face, Steve reengages by saying something like, "You will?" Then he takes another moment to pause before saying, "Thank you." In effect, Steve was showing the children that what they had to say mattered. Don't we all yearn for this?

I was that kid who couldn't sit any closer to the TV when *Mister Rogers' Neighborhood* was on. I nodded when Mister Rogers talked to me, I laughed when he laughed, and you can bet I answered him when he asked me a question. Mister Rogers was my friend. I believed him when he told me that he liked me just the way I was. The way Mister Rogers looked straight into the camera—and paused to listen—made me feel as if he was talking *just to me*. That pause gave me confidence. I felt both seen and heard.

TAKING A MOMENT IN REAL LIFE

THE POWER OF TAKING A MOMENT IN CONVERSATION:

Creating a pause between what is said and our response ensures that we are truly engaged in meaningful conversation. Interestingly, using the pause encourages a mirror effect: when we pause to process what other people are saying, they almost always pause too as they consider what you said. The pause, especially when it is deliberate and mindful, changes the energy in the room. You will find that the more you pause with intention, the better the atmosphere for caring, sharing, learning, and bonding.

THE POWER OF TAKING A MOMENT IN DECISION-MAKING:

Think of the pause as an "Add to Cart" strategy: a forced pause to make sure that what you are about to purchase is intentional, not an impulse buy. Similarly, when it comes to making a decision, pause. Sleep on it. Give it time.

I use this strategy before I say yes to more work or a trip or an invitation to a party. The pause gives me time and space to tune in, listen to myself, and see whether I have the bandwidth for this new commitment. I channel my inner Shonda Rhimes (the amazing producer and screenwriter of such iconic TV shows as *Grey's Anatomy* and *Station 19*) and think of her philosophy: "Every 'yes' changes something in me. Every 'yes' is a bit more transformative. Every 'yes' sparks some new phase of revolution." So when I do say yes, I better be ready for it.

When it comes to our children, the pause has a lot of competition. We don't always have time to take a lengthy pause each step along the way as we, say, help our toddler decide on a snack. But remind yourself that kids work at a different pace than adults. They deliberate over truly important decisions such as what to have for a snack. If you can slow down to see the world through the eyes of a child, you, too, will have time to celebrate even the small things—which is what LIFE CLUES is all about.

PRACTICE TAKING A MOMENT:

The next time you feel pressured to say yes, implement the pause. The pause gives us control. The pause gives us power. In fact, the magic of the pause is that it bolsters self-worth. When we pause for ourselves, we are happier because we are choosing relationships and situations that are more authentic, fulfilling, and rewarding.

Find <u>Your</u> Clues

**If you can take a trip down memory lane
and see what interested you,
that's at least a clue as to where
your interest may begin to develop.**

—ANGELA DUCKWORTH

I think I was always looking for my own clues. Case in point: When I was in high school I wrote a research paper about the man who became my mentor, Fred Rogers. I learned that he studied psychology, specifically, child development theory, and he used that knowledge to develop *Mister Rogers' Neighborhood*.

Doesn't seem like a big deal. We **all** write papers in school, but I really enjoyed doing the research for that report. I mean, *really*. Without knowing it, the time, the excitement, and the energy that went into writing that paper was a signal to what lay ahead in my life.

A few years later when I was in college, I started studying psychology and worked as a teacher's assistant in the preschool on campus. In the summer, I worked as a camp counselor in charge of all the preschoolers. After college, I studied child development and instructional technology and media. One way or another, I was always choosing to be with kids, learn about kids, and learn how I could educate them within the medium of television. When people asked what I wanted to do with a psychology degree, I proudly answered that I wanted to create a television show for kids.

Well, people laughed—not the reception I was expecting. No one believed that I could make a career out of creating television for kids. Even my father would roll his eyes and say something like, "A million people want to do what you want to do—why do you think it would be you?" I would choke back tears and think, "Why *wouldn't* it be me?"

And yet, my first show, *Blue's Clues*, premiered in 1996 to great acclaim. Millions of children tuned in every day to learn from and play along with the show. Years later, my father admitted he had been wrong, and I felt a wave of pride. But I was never prouder than when Fred Rogers himself looked me in the eye and told me that kids all over the world will be influenced by *Blue's Clues*, and that HE was proud of ME. Can you imagine the tingle of excitement that went down my spine? I can still feel it to this day!

Just as Blue the puppy leaves clues, the universe leaves clues for us. To me, *Blue's Clues* is not just a TV show for preschoolers; it's a metaphor for life. If you have a question, and you keep your eyes open, you will find your

If you have a question, and you keep your eyes open, you will find your answer because clues and answers are all around us.

answer because clues and answers are all around us. I'm not trying to be all woo-woo about this but the truth is, as adults, we tend to circle around the things we love. We read about topics we are interested in, we gravitate toward certain types of people who have certain ways of thinking and certain jobs that we find interesting. Our happiest memories, our most joyous moments, even the music we listen to are all clues to what makes us happy.

In her book *The Artist's Way* (which I mentioned in "A Note for You"), Julia Cameron coined the term "shadow artists" to describe people who circle around things they love but ignore the artist within them. Shadow artists were not supported in their early artistic endeavors by their family or people in their immediate circle. As a result, they do not believe or even know that they are artists. Sadly, they deny themselves their own creativity. Shadow artists ignore the clues all around them.

I did this at first, too. I told myself I was an academic. I wrote academic papers on how children learn from television and how we can use the influential nature of television to teach important skills through stories and game play. Then one day a colleague gave me Julia Cameron's book. Almost immediately, my life started to change because I could see my shadow artist self. I began to recount the clues in my life that had led me down each path. Right then and there, as I was coming home from work on the Metro-North train, I started writing. What I wrote on that day would become (after many drafts and collaborations) the pilot episode of *Blue's Clues*.

So how do we discover clues in our daily life? We find the clues by increasing our awareness. By becoming mindful of how we react to the world around us. We can start by remembering to look up from our phones every once in a while, because we never know where our next clue will pop up!

It also helps to focus on a positive viewpoint. A positive outlook will bring you closer to positive people, news, and clues. It expands our vision, enabling us to

> **A positive outlook will bring you closer to positive people, news, and clues.**

think of what could be. Our brain takes on what we think about, so when we revel in the positive, we attract positivity. For example, when we stand with our arms crossed, our brains automatically begin to channel anger. But when we smile, our brains channel happiness. Sounds simplistic, sure. But focusing on the negative will undoubtedly attract more of what you don't want in life.

FINDING YOUR CLUES IN THE REAL WORLD

SET THE STAGE FOR PAYING ATTENTION:

When you have a problem that keeps you up at night, how do you figure out what to do? You could ask for help. You could poll your friends. You could do a Google search. But the answer is within you; you just need to spot the clues. Take time every day to sit in a chair and let your body relax. Your mind might need some convincing to slow down, but you will find that when you rest your body, what's going on inside your head will slow down too. Oftentimes you already know the answer to the questions you're asking; you just need a moment to allow that insight to come through.

JOURNAL YOUR CLUES:

Get out your handy dandy notebook! There is so much information all around us that sometimes we need to write things down. Have you ever been stuck on a work problem, only to be suddenly inspired with the solution in the middle of a conversation about something utterly unrelated? That's because when we relax, we open ourselves to the wonders of life around us, including being open to resolutions that were eluding us.

Have you ever been asked a question, and gave an answer that you didn't realize was going to come out of your mouth? These are your clues! Take note. Write them down. If something feels like a sign, it generally is. Even if it seems like a small thing, if it's meaningful to you, write it down in your notebook. It doesn't matter what your notebook looks like; it could be the notes app on your phone or an old-school spiral-bound notebook. The important thing is to have a place where you can record your thoughts, and keep it with you at all times. Put it on your bedside table. Take it on the subway. Just like Steve, Joe, and Josh, you never know when a clue will appear. You want to be ready when it does.

CLUES IN PLAIN SIGHT:

Sometimes a clue will appear in something someone says. Sometimes it's in the words on a billboard or a literal sign on a signpost. I had a friend who was angry at her sister and didn't know what to do about her feelings. While she was driving home from her sister's, my friend made a left onto Mercy Street. Something about the word *mercy* hit home. My friend took a deep breath. She said the word out loud. Her question had been how she was going to react to her sister. The word *mercy* was a clue that led her to the answer: She would react with empathy and, of course, mercy. Her empathetic response made their relationship stronger.

Pay attention to the songs you listen to and the TV shows you binge. Listen for words that stand out in conversations. Maybe the word *fashion* keeps popping up on a podcast and in conversations with colleagues and friends. If it's grabbing your attention, it's possible that it means something for you. Maybe you're interested in learning more about the topic, or maybe you want to spruce up your wardrobe so that you feel more confident at work. These signposts that pop up in our lives are like little notes from the universe. They have something important to tell us.

Never Stop Playing

**The creation of something new
is not accomplished by the intellect but by the
play instinct acting from inner necessity.**

—CARL JUNG

I thoroughly believe in the power of play—for both kids and adults. The times when we are immersed in play, doing something we love, or laughing and being with friends and family, are the times when we learn the most about ourselves. When little ones play, they also let their guard down, open up, and reveal their true feelings.

At work, I focused on play, which helped me become someone the network trusted. At Nickelodeon, one of the favorite parts of my job was attending focus group sessions. A group of network executives, TV show creators, and I would sit behind a one-way mirror while a moderator talked with preschoolers about a new show that Nickelodeon was considering. During one of these sessions, I noticed that the group of five-year-olds was uncharacteristically lackluster. The kids were not communicating. The moderator struggled to get them to say anything at all. I watched as the moderator asked each child to rate the show he or she had just watched on a scale of 1 to 10 (a challenging task for any preschooler who's only just mastered the art of counting). None of the children responded until finally one little boy held up five fingers. "Five," he said. One by one, the other kids followed suit, each holding up their fingers and saying "five."

From the corner of my eye, I saw the show creator, who was sitting near me, slowly lower his head and start banging it quietly on the table. Clearly, he was upset. His show wasn't doing well in the market testing, and it was under intense scrutiny. He turned to me. "A five?" he said. His eyes were begging for help. "How could they give it a five? And why? Why did they give it a five?" This was exactly the question the moderator was asking the kids. But none of them answered, and it appeared that there was a standoff. The moderator was exasperated, as you can imagine you would be with a room full of preschoolers who were done with you. She stepped out and poked her head in our room. She asked if we had any other questions we'd like to ask. I did. Could I introduce myself as a "special guest" and ask the children a few questions about the show? The moderator was only too happy for the reprieve, and I headed to the other side of the one-way glass.

After introducing myself, I sat down on the floor, met the kids at their level, made eye contact, and began to play. For ten minutes that's all we did—play. There were toys all **around**. We played blocks and action figures, and we laughed. One preschooler brought me a cup of pretend tea, which I drank. Another child, who was dressed from head to toe in a Princess Jasmine outfit, started working a pretend hairbrush through my hair. I decided to ask her about the show. "Princess Jasmine," I said, "did you like the show you just watched?" She answered, "Yes! It was funny! And so cute!" She continued brushing my hair. After a pause, I asked, "Well, then, Princess Jasmine, why did you give the show a five?"

Then something magical happened. Princess Jasmine scooched really close to me, perhaps because she didn't want me to miss hearing what she had to say, which she delivered with astonishing forcefulness.

"Because I'm five!" She held up five fingers to drive the point home. "And I loved that show!" The rest of my new preschool friends piped up. They told me that they had all given the show a five because they were five years old. Preschool reasoning at its finest!

Using play to continue our interactions, I discovered that not only did the children understand the storyline, but they also liked the characters enough to act out the show for me. They sang the songs they

Kids have the right idea: a play mindset leads to more happiness.

had heard, and they retold their favorite jokes.

I said goodbye to the preschoolers and went back to the other side of the one-way glass. The grateful creator of the show enveloped me in a warm hug. Play had saved the day and the creator's dream of making *Allegra's Window* a reality. And, by the way, it got me a promotion, too.

As adults, it might seem odd to say we should make play a priority. After all, we inhabit a serious world. Turn on the news or scroll through social media and you'll be reminded instantly just how serious it is. Yet there is a deep connection between play and happiness.

Kids have the right idea: a play mindset leads to more happiness. Science backs up this statement. According to a 2017 *Washington Post* article by Jennifer Wallace, "Why It's Good for Grownups to Go Play," play has been found to "speed up learning, enhance productivity and increase job satisfaction." Dr. Stuart Brown, founder of the National Institute for Play, adds, "Play is a basic human need as essential to our well-being as sleep, so when we're low on play, our minds and bodies notice. We need to incorporate play into our everyday lives." I couldn't agree more.

Let's talk for a minute about a common experience. Let's say you are at lunch with a new group of colleagues, and everyone is looking at his or her phone. It feels uncomfortable. Well, be playful! Introduce an icebreaker game. Ask everyone to name a favorite animal or a favorite kind of food. You'll be surprised at how freely people will participate.

Changing your mindset toward play takes practice. It may not come naturally to you. Our inherent ability to play has been conditioned out of us by the time we enter the workforce. But I promise: It won't be long before you will start to see *and feel* the joy of being in the game.

It takes courage to choose a playful mindset and to take a small step toward that mindset, but the rewards are worth it.

PLAYFULNESS IN REAL LIFE

REINVENT PLAYTIME:

To unlock the power of play in your daily life, start by embracing a playful mindset. Shift your perspective and approach tasks, challenges, and interactions with a lighthearted attitude. See the world through the lens of curiosity and wonder, eagerly embracing new experiences that come your way.

Additionally, seek out activities that bring you joy and ignite your playful spirit. Whether it's engaging in sports, pursuing hobbies, exploring your creative side, dancing, or playing a musical instrument, find what sparks your interest and allows you to have fun. Prioritize these activities by setting aside dedicated leisure time in your schedule. Treat play as a vital component of your overall well-being, just like sleep and exercise. Make room for recreational pursuits that bring you happiness and help you unwind.

GET GOOD AT PRETENDING:

Remember when we did this all the time as kids? We can do this as adults. One example: Maybe you're not a baker, but you can pretend to be a pastry chef who is baking the most delectable cookies that have ever come out of an oven. You can even have your own pretend baking show! Even if the recipe doesn't turn out as well as you hoped, the aromas wafting through your house are rewarding enough to make the whole endeavor worth your effort!

And you don't have to bake alone either. Call a friend, or pull your toddler into it because doing anything with a young person can be a marvelous adventure. Baking with a toddler is a surefire way to take the pressure of "perfect" and toss it right out the window! Two weeks or two years from now, will anyone remember how dry that loaf of banana bread was? Probably not. But even if you do, you'll be able to laugh about it because it was created through shared playtime.

PLAY ICEBREAKER GAMES:

Okay, so I'll admit that icebreakers at the start of a work meeting or a social situation can feel . . . well, forced. Forced fun is the worst. Or is it? Maybe the key is to call it out for what it is. Admitting the obvious can dissipate a lot of tension. Make an announcement: "We're going to get some conversation going. Let's start with an icebreaker. I know, I know, none of us love the idea of icebreakers, and it's going to feel forced at first, but just humor me, please. Just go with it." And then get everyone going with an icebreaking game.

Always Try to Find Something Good

How great it is when we come to know
that times of disappointment can be followed
by times of fulfillment; that sorrow can be
followed by joy; that guilt over falling short
of our ideals can be replaced by pride
in doing all that we can; and that anger can be
channeled into creative achievements . . .
and into dreams that we can make come true.

—FRED ROGERS

When something seems bad,
turn it around and find something good.

—DANIEL TIGER'S NEIGHBORHOOD

In my early twenties, I was a waitress with a dream. That dream was to work at *Sesame Street*. For years, I had dreamed about working there, and so I applied for a position. But it wasn't meant to be. I remember the chipper voice on the other end of the phone telling me that I didn't get the job. Then she chirped something about good luck and wished me well.

I hung up the phone and cried. In that moment, it felt like all my dreams were going up in flames. Clearly, I was destined to forever be a waitress with flair.

After a few days of mourning the loss of something I'd longed for, I took a non-paying internship on a pre-school series. The show was called *Eureeka's Castle*, and the production company, Noyes & Laybourne, was in New York City. My tips from waitressing barely covered the bus fare from New Jersey. However, this was me hoping to find something good in my crushing disappointment.

This wasn't *Sesame Street*, but I soon learned that it had something even better: the new and wildly creative network of Nickelodeon in the 1990s. That internship blossomed into the friendship and mutual admiration of two people who changed my life: Kit Laybourne, producer and founder of the company, and Geraldine Laybourne, president of Nickelodeon, who was and still is regarded as a visionary in children's media. It also led to a job in the research department at Nickelodeon. Because the network was new, the team encouraged out-of-the-box thinking and creativity. Soon, I found myself living a whole new life post-disappointment. I was back on track. Five years later, I had the greatest opportunity of my life to write a pilot for *Blue Prints*, which later became *Blue's Clues*.

> **My personal journey reminds me that disappointment is not the end of the story.**

My personal journey reminds me that disappointment is not the end of the story. In her book of the same name, Professor Angela Duckworth defines "grit" as "the ability to pursue your goals with passion and perseverance as if they are a marathon, not a sprint." Duckworth goes on to say that in the face of adversity, resilience and patience are essential to success.

My dream was to show relatable stories of conflict, adversity, and strong emotions in order to model problem-solving through empathy, grit, and resilience. Building these skills in children would set kids up to use them as adults. Disappointment was the theme of the first story I wrote for *Daniel Tiger's Neighborhood.* Daniel was super excited about his birthday and wanted to decorate his own birthday cake. Proud of his cake decorating, Daniel insisted on carrying the cake home. But a preschooler excitedly bouncing his cake up and down in its bakery box as he rides a trolley home was a recipe for disappointment. Sure enough, the cake is smushed, and Daniel is crushed.

This is a critical moment. The children watching little Daniel Tiger were feeling his emotions. I even saw a few tears falling when we did a test run of the show. When Daniel is able to gather himself, he asks, "What would you do if you were disappointed?" Dad Tiger sings the strategy in a song. "When something seems bad, turn it around and find something good." Dad Tiger asks Daniel to find something good in the disaster. But Daniel's got nothing.

As I wrote this script, it was important to me that Daniel didn't come up with the solution right away. One of my goals was to reinforce the concept that dealing with experiences like disappointment is a process. So the next step in the process is to let Dad Tiger help his little cub.

But how? What could we write that would help kids understand how they can find the silver lining in a challenging situation? So we literally decided to bake a cake. We smushed the cake. We ate the cake. And you know what? IT STILL TASTED DELICIOUS. We discovered the positive side. We decided to add this experience to the episode. We had Daniel Tiger sample the cake. Then he exclaimed, "Cakes taste yummy, even when they're smushy!"

This marked the initial step in conveying the lesson. However, both Daniel and the young ones watching from home needed more examples. So we used our imaginations and explored the concept in future episodes. In one show, Daniel finds the silver lining in a picnic washed out by rain; in another, he uncovers the good in a canceled play date. With each disappointing event, Daniel sang the same song and highlighted something positive.

The key takeaway here is HOW we handle disappointment, which serves as a vital LIFE CLUE. The more honest and patient we are with the sadness, frustration, and anger accompanying disappointment, the more we realize that these emotions resemble waves that eventually pass over us. Once the wave of emotion recedes, we can regain our footing and see the bright side of what just happened. Each step in the process helps **us** work our way toward a resolution.

FINDING THE GOOD IN REAL LIFE

FEEL ALL THE FEELS:

Fred Rogers gave wise counsel when he said, "What is mentionable is manageable." In other words, sometimes you have to say what you're feeling. Of course, this means we have to get clear on what we are feeling. Gaining this clarity takes time and requires introspection. This is why I love the list of emotions formulated by bestselling author Brené Brown. Google her list of 87 Human Emotions and Experiences—you'll thank her afterward.

Words are powerful. It's like they carry an electric charge. And the better we are at describing what we feel, the better we become at directing our energy and understanding our truth. When things don't go as planned, Brown suggests using words like *regret, discouragement,* and *frustration* to help clarify or identify what you might be feeling. When we fall short of our expectations, we might experience shame or embarrassment. Using this list to name what we are feeling might not cure everything, but it's a good first step in overcoming adversity. When I didn't get that job at Sesame Street, I felt discouraged, insecure, and fearful, which led to my sadness and disillusionment. Chalk it up to youthful tenacity, but I'm glad I was able to articulate these feelings and understand where I was emotionally. So I persevered. I took a step forward.

LOCATE A LIFE VEST:

Riding through a wave of disappointment starts with confidence and the cultivation of resilience. Every problem, no matter how big or small, can be handled. Knowing that you have a life vest will allow you to keep your head above water. Our life vests come in all sizes, too. Some examples: I keep protein bars (always the chocolate ones!) in my bag. It started with emergency snacks for the kids, but I kept it going for myself. My girlfriends and I call an "all hands on" dinner when one of us is going through something. We know that when we get that text, we need to make time for one another. And it has truly saved us. Of course, there are small problems and scary frights. But then there are the catastrophic events like when you or someone you love gets a cancer scare. I'm not suggesting grit and determination will solve the problem. But I am suggesting that reaching out to family and friends for a life vest may help you get through it. The point is, don't go it alone. Create a life vest for yourself but also ask for help, being specific about what you need. Find the care you need and create the environment that will help you heal.

FIND THE WIN IN THE SWIM:

For preschoolers, their problems are big to them, and they handle their feelings loudly! They throw themselves on the floor and wail or stomp their feet when they're angry. I love this outpouring of emotion because as we age, our emotions get suppressed, but the feelings are still there. What should we do? We need to pick ourselves up, dust ourselves off, and get back in the game. Sink or swim. Keep your head above water and when you make it to the shore, don't forget to appreciate the win that was in the swim.

We all experience powerful feelings from time to time, but the greatest growth comes when we acknowledge those big feelings. If we can label those feelings, and use strategies to help ourselves cope with them, we can stay afloat. Simple? Maybe. But don't underestimate simple. Simple works.

Use Your Mind

When you use your mind, take a step at a time; you can do anything that you wanna do.

—BLUE'S CLUES

I wholeheartedly embrace the idea of "paws-itive" goal-setting. By this I mean defining what we want and then methodically taking action that moves us toward our dreams and desires. Goal-setting is so crucial that we even composed a toe-tapping melody that is sung on every episode of *Blue's Clues*, and paired it with the lyrics shown above in this chapter's epigraph. It's all about focus + action! While initially intended for preschoolers, the advice in this song holds true for adults as well. When we engage our minds by exploring new ideas, asking questions, conducting thorough research, and approaching our goals in a step-by-step manner, we can cultivate a success-oriented mindset that propels us toward success.

But, for us adults, this seemingly simple strategy is often overlooked. Sometimes we **believe** we can't achieve what we want to achieve, so we give up before we even try. Sometimes we hear a silent "no" and don't even ask the question. Sometimes we are stressed, and all of our planning and research goes out the window. Sometimes instead of focusing our minds positively, we're all over the place.

I know this to be true because I've been there. When we showcased our pilot episode of *Blue's Clues*, the response from Nickelodeon decision-makers wasn't what we had hoped for. They criticized its slow pace, its basic cut-out animation, and even our choice to include talking salt and pepper shakers! My heart sank. It looked like Nickelodeon was about to pass on our passion project, and my dream was on the brink of extinction.

While adults might have perceived the show's basic elements as missteps, we firmly believed in the magical qualities of the show. The deliberate pacing was designed to encourage kids to interact, the simple animation resembled a storybook, and characters like Mr. Salt and Mrs. Pepper were comedic gold to our target audience. To validate our instincts, we presented the episode to fifty preschoolers. Their response was electric. They fully engaged with the show, eagerly searching for clues, learning about colors, shapes, and even some elementary geometry.

Armed with this insight, we decided to record and visually convey the children's reactions. We filmed them as they watched the pilot, then juxtaposed that footage with the episode itself. This split screen, showcasing young viewers immersed in the content and actively participating, was our key to unlocking the potential of *Blue's Clues* for Nickelodeon executives. Their doubts were erased by irrefutable evidence of the show's appeal to its intended audience.

Perceptions shifted when the split screen images were shown at that executive meeting. As they watched the kids' reactions side by side with the content, they began to understand. The show wasn't too slow; it was perfectly attuned to its young viewers. Thanks to this demonstration, we earned the green light for a full first season, laying the groundwork for ten unforgettable seasons.

Use your mind is a LIFE CLUE because it represents the distillation of learning from everything—disappointments, failures, successes, and interpersonal interactions. According to Dr. Dashun Wang and his colleagues at Northwestern University, failure is an "essential prerequisite for success." These researchers found that "every winner begins as a loser but not every failure leads to success." They were able to isolate why. People who eventually succeeded did so not because of the number of attempts they made. Rather, success was determined by using their minds to work smarter and incorporate lessons learned from their mistakes. Those who worked "smarter not harder" became the success stories.

Simply trying again may not get us anywhere. But if we mindfully apply insights we've learned from our mistakes, we can use this new awareness to catapult us to the success we desire.

> Simply trying again may not get us anywhere. But if we mindfully apply insights we've learned from our mistakes, we can use this new awareness to catapult us to the success we desire.

Flexing this thinking muscle is so important that we use the game show format on *Blue's Clues* for kids to practice making smaller decisions with a clear mind. On the show, when Blue wants something, she leaves behind clever clues. Initially, neither Steve, Joe, or Josh know what she wants. But by following the clues one step at a time, the answer reveals itself. It's a process that highlights determination and problem-solving skills. Blue's best friend never gives up, knowing that a solution will always be found, even if it requires some time and effort.

All of this reminds us of the profound impact our own handling of failure has on those around us. It highlights the importance of being resilient, persistent, and thoughtful in our decision-making processes. By embracing the mindset of trying new things, taking small steps toward our goals, and learning from mistakes, we create an environment in which those around us, especially our children, can witness and then mirror these qualities. As adults, we must be aware that, for better or for worse, we are always being observed. When we demonstrate resilience, persistence, and optimism by navigating the stages of stumbling, analyzing, and turning failures into opportunities, we provide a powerful example for others.

USING YOUR MIND IN REAL LIFE

FIGURE OUT WHAT YOU WANT:

Start this process by doing a personal inventory. Ask yourself: Who am I? What do I love to do? Do I love working with kids or am I craving adult companionship? What are my strengths, and who might benefit from me sharing these strengths? If you're an avid reader, the library might be a good place to start. Are there local schools in need of reading tutors? Do you want to meet active people your own age? Maybe joining a pickleball club would be a good way to spend your time.

LEARN BY OBSERVING:

What does using your mind in real life look like? Let's consider a couple of scenarios. You've moved to a new neighborhood, and you want to get to know your new neighbors, but you're shy. What can you do? First, observe. Are your neighbors primarily parents of young kids, or are their children in high school? If the kids are little, the parents are probably just as eager as you are to get together. Plan a coffee break after the bus has carted the kids off to school. All you need is hot coffee and tea, some pastries, and a genuine interest in getting to know the community you just moved into.

If this is a neighborhood with teenagers, nothing will make your new neighbors feel better than being able to share their child's journey with someone else who's interested. Go to the local high school's football games and cheer for the kid down the street who's playing junior varsity. Go to your neighbor's daughter's band concert if her grandparents live out of state. Their parents will think you're an earth angel.

FREEDOM TO FAIL:

It can be difficult to stand by and watch as loved ones make mistakes. However, there is value in experiencing setbacks and facing the consequences of their actions. Tough love, but tough love with compassion. Unless immediate harm is involved, it's better in the long run to let them learn from their choices. These moments of struggle are where genuine growth happens. Granting loved ones the freedom to face outcomes is a gift that promotes self-esteem. One of the privileges of being an adult is that we can provide a safety net so that when our loved ones are experimenting with how to succeed at life, the consequences of failing are not catastrophic. We are able to be supportive at the same time as we give them the freedom to navigate their own consequences. These are some of the most powerful lessons that will impart wisdom and resilience. We're here to cheer them on every step of the way as they learn and grow!

And guess what? This applies to us as well! Making mistakes is both normal and necessary. It's crucial that we learn from our choices, take responsibility for the consequences, and then simply carry on.

Take It One Step at a Time

One step at a time is all it takes to get you there.

—EMILY DICKINSON

Have you ever stared at a blank page with fear? I remember when I was given the immense privilege of creating an animated show to honor Fred Rogers' legacy. How could I even begin?

Well, I didn't. I stared at a blank page . . . FOR HOURS!

The little blinking cursor seemed to be taunting me to write something that was worthy of my real-life hero, professional mentor, and beloved friend.

My husband, bless his heart, saved me from my paralysis. "Just take it one step at a time," he said with a smirk.

I took a pause. Then I laughed at myself for not remembering to use my own philosophy.

And that is exactly what I did. I wrote one word. *Daniel*. Then another. *Tiger*. *Daniel Tiger*. There it was: the beginning, using my favorite character from the original series as the preschool embodiment of Mister Rogers.

It was the beginning in two ways. First, it was the beginning of the animated show that Fred Rogers Productions had invited me to create. Second, it took me all the way back to the beginning of my life. When I was a small child who was star-struck by Mister Rogers, my favorite character on the show was Daniel Tiger. Perhaps unsurprisingly, then, this character manifested himself in this tribute. My two opening words, *Daniel Tiger*, presented themselves as the young son of the Daniel Tiger that had prowled Mister Rogers' neighborhood.

> When attempting something that is new or more challenging, just take it step-by-step.

This animated little Daniel began to come alive **in** my imagination. He wore—no surprise here—a red sweater and blue Keds sneakers. (I may as well have named him Fred Junior.) Little Daniel—again, no surprise here—looked right straight at the camera. He smiled. And then he "rubbed noses" with the children at home and said, "Ugga Mugga," a phrase made famous in the original Mister Rogers series. Before I knew it, my concept filled several pages of typewritten development, and there was no looking back.

One step at a time, one word at a time, one day at a time—that's how little Daniel Tiger was born.

In writing children's programming, our goal is to engage kids. We begin with something that all kids love: Play. We play a game that involves a concept they are likely to know. Something like, say, colors. We then break it down. We start with one of the primary colors and then introduce other colors one at a time. We gradually increase the level of difficulty from, say, yellow to turquoise to chartreuse. That process of building from the familiar to the unfamiliar never fails to keep kids engaged and learning every step of the way.

The same dynamics are at work in the adult world. When attempting something that is new or more challenging, just take it step-by-step. It's what we do when we're teaching our kids to ride a bike: We start with training wheels. As the child develops competence, confidence, and a little bit of muscle memory, the training wheels come off. Freedom and fun follow.

So where do you begin when you want to start something new? You begin with one step. Then every time you feel overwhelmed, you remind yourself that all you have to do is take one more step. This is not the time to take the long view. When you are attempting something that is unknown or intimidating, it's better to keep a micro-view of the task. Don't worry about all the steps it will take for you to get to your goal. Just worry about the next one.

TAKING IT ONE STEP AT A TIME IN REAL LIFE

ONE STEP, ONE MINUTE:

When you take life one step at a time, try getting through the next minute, and then breathe. Before you know it, you have gotten through the next hour, which turns into the next day. Little by little, you are going toward the next day at work or the next school meeting, or you have gotten through the next illness or family crisis. Try bite-size pieces, breathe, rejoice in your accomplishments, and then you can decide what to do next.

WORK PARALYSIS—ONE SMALL PART AT A TIME:

When kids are too overwhelmed to clean their outrageously messy rooms, what unfreezes their paralysis? Just pick up one toy and then one book. When homework seems too hard? Do one assignment at a time. It's the same for us adults. Overwhelmed by your schedule? Take it one hour at a time. Overwhelmed by learning something new? Do a little bit every day. Juggling too many projects at work or at home? Break it down and attack one aspect at a time.

CELEBRATE THE SMALL JOYS:

I truly believe that we must celebrate the small joys in life. Just like on *Blue's Clues*, where we celebrate when the mail comes, stop and sing every time your favorite song comes on Spotify. Better yet, take those three minutes to DANCE! Taking it one step at a time also means making a mountain out of a molehill. That's right: I want you to make a mountain, not the other way around! Don't wait to celebrate only the big milestones; celebrate the little ones, too. Did your daughter ride her bike for a few minutes before falling over? Hurray! Did your son learn a new song on the piano? That deserves its own cake!

You Can Do Anything You Wanna Do

Don't wait for the right opportunity: create it.

—GEORGE BERNARD SHAW

I believe wholeheartedly that we should be driven by passion toward what we want to do. Along the way, however, you may encounter your own LIFE CLUES that may alter your life journey and create a new dream. Here's how it happened to me: After high school, I went to college to study pre-med. I wanted to help people, and I thought the way to do this was to be a doctor. Given my great love for children and my interest in childhood, I considered specializing in child psychiatry. I took the required classes and interned at a hospital for children with mental health issues. I dove into the work and became obsessed with helping them.

When it came to my own life, however, I was disconnected, pessimistic, and unmotivated. I was uninvested in my classes. My friends sat me down and suggested that I figure out a way that I could still help kids, only not as a pre-med student.

It would have been easy to interpret my friends' intervention as a sign of failure. But I gave their well-intentioned advice some thought, and it led me to select a radically different course load for the next semester. These new classes stoked my passion rather than my fear. I was *excited* to get to class; I gobbled up everything that had to do with child development, educational theory, and the influential nature of children's television. I joined the psychology club. When I learned that one of my friends would be working at *Sesame Street* after her graduation, it was like a light bulb exploded inside my mind. I hustled over to the career center, asked a million questions, and researched the field.

The fire was lit; I could help millions of kids through television!

Everything I did from that point on was designed to get me closer to my goal. I earned a master's degree in child development. What I learned was poured into a capstone project, my master's thesis, which became the PBS television show *Super Why!*

You either grow up believing you can, or you grow up believing you can't. I am here to tell you that it's better to believe you can. Will you be an Olympic gold medalist in gymnastics? Maybe not. But if you love gymnastics, and you devote **yourself** to being whatever kind of gymnast you can be, your efforts can bring you joy and satisfaction. Like a flower bending toward the sun, leaning toward your joy and passion will make all the difference in your life. You will be much more likely to fashion the kind of outcome that matches your dream.

. . . leaning toward your joy and passion will make all the difference in your life. You will be much more likely to fashion the kind of outcome that matches your dream.

In all my shows, I want to give kids a reason to believe that they can dream—and do. The games on *Blue's Clues* are designed to have children practice the skills that will help them learn, strategize, and make decisions. We created cognitive games that focus on the essential components of a kindergarten readiness curriculum: reading, math, deduction skills, patterning, and socialization. Through our scripts, we made successive layers of each game more challenging.

YOU CAN DO ANYTHING YOU WANNA DO IN REAL LIFE

PRACTICE CONFIDENCE:

The truth is, we can rewire our brain to believe we are confident before we actually are. The trick is simple but powerful: Literally tell yourself you can do it. You can say it to yourself as you walk down the street or to your reflection in a mirror as you hype yourself up. I told myself that I was going to create my own TV show so often that when it really happened, I was a bit gobsmacked. The point is: Be your own advocate. Don't let in the voices of your naysayers.

PUT YOURSELF ON YOUR TO-DO LIST:

Adults often neglect self-care due to busy schedules and pressing responsibilities. Prioritize self-care activities by scheduling them on your calendar or adding them to your to-do list. Whether it's going for a walk, reading a book, or taking a relaxing bath, these activities should be treated as important tasks that deserve your time and attention.

PROTECT YOUR SELF-WORTH:

As someone who has (mostly) recovered from low self-esteem, I value this LIFE CLUE above all others. Whenever I try something new and fail, I remind myself how many failures it took to reach my dream. As someone who suffers from people pleasing, I want everyone to like me and see my contributions, but it doesn't work that way. You have to please yourself and know your own worth in order to reflect it back into the world. Every time I do something new, and someone tilts their head and says, "Well, it's never been done that way before," that's my sign that I'm on the right track.

So use your mind, take it one step at a time, and do anything that you wanna do. I believe in you.

Cultivate Routines

**See the world as if for the first time;
see it through the eyes of a child,
and you will suddenly find that you are free.**

—DEEPAK CHOPRA

Do you **remember** what it felt like to be a child? To have space to play, practice, rest, and learn. There were moments during which we were encouraged to physically run around, and there were moments to slow down and get creative with a paintbrush. There were moments to clean up and do our chores, and there were moments for rest and naptime. Research shows that consistent routines and daily rituals help cultivate strong social and emotional development in children. As adults, most of us have some sort of routine, but what if we directed those routines in the direction of fun?

Here's what I mean: Consider what you loved and needed when you were a kid. Was it playtime? Space for creating art? Time to read and imagine? Identify what you loved most as a child and begin injecting these things into your daily activities. This might mean taking time during your busy day to do something you love. Text a friend at 11:30 a.m. every day, or add a short walk after lunch to your routine of eating lunch at 1:00 p.m., or send a playful emoji to your spouse or partner every day when you're waiting to pick up the kids or standing on a train platform waiting for your ride home. Make your daily ritual of drinking tea or sparkling water something special by being deliberate about actually enjoying your beverage of choice. Appreciating a sip of water can be fun if you're living with an attitude of enjoying the people and things around you. Too often, we miss what we do during the day (not to mention the people we see every day) because our heads are filled with chatter and our bodies are filled with nervous energy. But when we put our focus on something, we turn a mundane experience into something sacred and special.

I fully admit that I'm the type of person who can get wrapped up in all I have to do during the day:

getting the kids ready for school and myself ready for work, putting in long hours, and taking care of my family in the evenings. But I try to keep in mind the words of my dear friend Fred Rogers and inject a little fun into my routines: "Play is the real work of childhood." Now, granted Fred didn't say, "Play is the real work of adulthood," but I believe he would agree that we are all children at heart and should never abandon playfulness even when we exchange a sandbox for school, family, and a career.

Preschoolers' days are full of routines and little rituals that help them feel safe and grounded. That's why so many children's television shows follow a similar format. In *Blue's Clues*, we sang about the mail on every show. Our friend Mailbox delivering the mail was as reliable as the sun rising in the morning. To celebrate this joyous little event, we sang and danced every time we received a letter. (Sometimes, I still do!) To signal the closing of each day, we sang songs to celebrate the time we spent together, such as the "So Long Song" we have been singing on *Blue's Clues* for twenty years. On *Daniel Tiger's Neighborhood*, Daniel Tiger imagines something that took place in every episode, and says a sweet "Ugga Mugga" ("I love you") before saying goodbye.

We live in an unpredictable world, but human beings are creatures of habit. Most of us thrive with positive routines. When we know what to expect, we can relax into the day. This allows us to remain calm, take control of our environment, and become more receptive to learning and experimenting. It even encourages us to occasionally shake up our routines! For example, if your habit is to brush your teeth every morning promptly at 6:30, maybe try brushing your teeth with your nondominant hand. I'm left-handed, so brushing my teeth with my right hand is a bit of a challenge. Still, I keep my overarching routines in place and make small changes, what my friend Gary Jansen calls "microshifts," every now and then

> *A daily plan can shape our days and be transformative for adults just like routines and rituals do for children.*

just to shake things up. And kids find these small changes exciting and fun. Breakfast for dinner? It's one of the easiest microshifts you can do with kids. And they love it!

A daily plan can shape our days and be transformative for adults just like routines and rituals do for children. "A ritual is a carefully selected way of doing something that has a sense of purpose and a positive side effect in addition to the straightforward completion of the task," writes Lucy Gower, trainer and consultant on innovation and bestselling author. "Rituals," she adds, "are internally motivated . . . and can provide energy and enjoyment along with efficiency and structure." In other words, rituals are routines that attain special significance from their inherent moments of sacredness.

Taking a page from our preschool selves, what if we made sure we established rituals around the basics of our own self-care, with snack time, nap time, bath time, and bedtime rituals?

ROUTINES AND RITUALS IN REAL LIFE

FIND THE TIME FOR SNACKS:

Few things are more important to little ones than snack time. Snacks provide a break from the day and keep children energized and focused. The same applies for us. Snacking not only boosts our energy, but taking a break for a little sustenance can also provide a small space for grace, a moment to reflect on what's been going on during the day or what's to come in the hours ahead.

In the first episode of *Blue's Clues*, we took twenty-two minutes to figure out what Blue wanted for a snack. This was intentional. Snacks are *that* important, and we wanted to get this point across to children and adults alike. We also wanted to address the bad rap that snacking sometimes gets, as if snacks are always unhealthy for you. "There is absolutely nothing wrong with snacking. It's the type of food you snack on that can help you maintain your mood, mental clarity, and metabolism," says Amy Lee, M.D., a board-certified physician specializing in internal medicine and member of the National Board of Physician Nutrition Specialists. Make snacking a daily routine. It's good for your mind and keeps the crabby moods away.

EAT MINDFULLY:

And speaking of food, paying attention to the foods you eat is a good routine to cultivate. Get to know your food better. Perhaps shop at a local farmers market and meet the people who grow the basil, tomatoes, lettuce, and cucumbers that will go into your salad. Knowing where your food comes from fosters a mindful moment! Create a colorful, pretty plate of green vegetables, purple eggplant, and red tomatoes. Then take time to savor the meal and enjoy the company around you. This will add happiness to your day that you didn't know was missing!

WHEN YOU ARE TIRED, TAKE A NAP:

No shame in a power nap. Just like we need to learn to eat when we are hungry and drink water when we are thirsty, we should become comfortable with resting when we are tired. Naps are good for the brain, which is why young children need to nap every day. (See: Kids have a lot to teach us!) While it's not 100 percent clear what happens to us when we sleep or why we need to sleep in the first place, naps clear out brain toxins that can make us unfocused or unmotivated.

Still, many adults see naps as a cop-out. Naps are good for a cranky child but a waste of precious time for adults. Not true. As Dr. Michael J. Breus, PhD, stated in *Psychology Today*, "There's a stubborn perception that napping is a sign of laziness. In fact, it's just the opposite. People who get the most out of napping are very driven and highly motivated. They want to get ahead, and they know that sleep plays a big part in performing at their best in daily life—at work, in relationships, in tackling challenges and goals, both physical and mental." Bottom line: Naps increase alertness, improve concentration, help us make better decisions, and enhance memory and learning. Take a nap.

Blue, Skidoo— You Can, Too!

Just try new things. Get out of your comfort zones and soar, all right?

—MICHELLE OBAMA

Our word for immersing ourselves into a new adventure by doing something new or taking a trip is "skidoo," and no matter what kind of skidoo it is— big or small—it is always exciting. One day when our daughters were four and six years old, my husband and I woke them at 4:30 in the morning. We plunked them into the car in their pajamas. They didn't know it yet, but we were headed for the airport. This is when we surprised them with the news that we were going on vacation. Of course, they squealed with delight. I was sitting in the back between the girls when the little one reached over and grabbed my hand. "Right NOW," she said, "right HERE, this is the best vacation ever!" We hadn't even left the driveway.

It's the unexpected that catches our attention and stands out in our memories. It doesn't matter if you actually go anywhere—what matters is that you used **your** imagination to "take" everyone somewhere together and do something new. The idea behind "Blue, skidoo, we can, too!" moments is to wonder. *What would it be like to jump inside a chalk board? What would the world look like?* Or, it is immersing ourselves in a new place and being curious to learn everything about it. But the real magic is what we skidoo together. On *Blue's Clues*, either Steve, Joe, or Josh follows Blue somewhere new so that they too can be part of the experience. During these adventures of spending time together and doing something new (or, if not new, something you enjoy), bonds are strengthened. Find your skidoo in your own life! Doing something different increases positivity and allows your loved ones to bond with you through new shared experiences.

The best gift we can give ourselves and our family and friends is the gift of time together. Positive, loving relationships are crucial for well-being across life; time spent together literally lengthens people's lives, providing resources that can help an individual cope with stress, engage in healthy behaviors, and enhance self-esteem.

When it comes to family, experts suggest spending money on vacations rather than toys. The positive memories last longer. "Family holidays are valued by children, both in the moment and for long afterward in their memory," says psychologist and best-

Doing something different increases positivity and allows your loved ones to bond with you through new shared experiences.

selling author Oliver James. "It's all about talking nonsense with your parents, sharing an ice cream and moments of time in which your interests are genuinely taken into account." The same principle applies to our besties, too. Sometimes a special dinner, day trip, or get-away with close friends can bring us so much happiness.

Spending time with friends and family also benefits our brains. "An enriched environment offers new experiences that are strong in combined social, physical, cognitive, and sensory interaction," says psychotherapist Dr. Margot Sunderland. It's true. Even if a vacation is out of the question, we can plan a staycation and explore our hometown: browse the library, meet vendors at a local farmers market, or stop by the ice cream parlor. As Dr. Sunderland notes, experiences like these affect the firing of brain neurons, "enhancing executive functions like stress regulation, attention, concentration, good planning, and the ability to learn, and also improving physical and mental health."

The bottom line is that spending time with your family and friends is good for body and mind.

So let's ALL skidoo!

SKIDOOING IN REAL LIFE

CREATE YOUR OWN BRAND OF SKIDOO:

What does skidooing in real life look like for you? Good question—and it really does differ from person to person. Finding your own skidoo is a little bit like doing investigative journalism. If you have little ones, watch them play. When they play, they are acting out their fantasies. If they play baker over and over again, then a trip to the bakery or having them bake with you in real life is a wonderful, personal skidoo! For the grown-ups, listen closely to the stories that people tell at parties. I've learned a lot by really leaning into what excites people. When someone wants to show me pictures, I'm intrigued; I want to see what they want to share. Do they like to travel? Does that inspire you to travel as well? Do they find satisfaction in volunteering? That might be a skidoo choice for you and your loved ones, too.

LIVE IN THE MOMENT:

The smallest things can excite children—a ladybug on the ground, a lawn sprinkler on a hot day, sidewalk chalk. Kids aren't worrying about deadlines or bills or having to drive home in traffic. They're focused on the here and now. They're not looking to the future or crying over the past. We can learn a lot from that mindset. Now, I'm not saying we toss away our responsibilities, but what if you collected lightning bugs on a hot summer night, or just walked barefoot on the grass, or went out for a drive in the evening to listen to your favorite music on your car stereo? Creating a skidoo in the present moment will bring you joy as you slow down, look at things with fresh eyes, and celebrate the small things.

CREATE ADVENTURES:

Adventures together are a better investment than putting your money into shiny new things. Invest your time, energy, and money in a family vacation, and make priceless, lifelong memories. Or go on an adventure with new foods, either by preparing a new recipe, trying a new restaurant, taking cooking classes, or starting a neighborhood foodie club. When we let go of daily tasks and chores, what we get in return is a myriad of gifts—memories, laughs, hugs—that last a lifetime.

Imagine, Every Day

**I am enough of an artist to draw freely upon
my imagination. Imagination is more important
than knowledge. Knowledge is limited.
Imagination encircles the world.**

—ALBERT EINSTEIN

As a child, my escape was books. I read book after
book imagining that I was the heroine in all the stories.
I was Harriet in *Harriet the Spy*, I was Charlie in the
fantastical world of *Charlie and the Chocolate Factory*.
I was "the one" in Danielle Steel romance novels. I
was the heroine who succeeded against all odds to
become a business tycoon/scientist/world-renowned
author.

I look back on those imaginative stories and see
how important it is to get lost in a dream world—to
go on an imaginary journey or adventure. Dreaming is
a creative endeavor, and when I dreamed, I chronicled

them. I wrote down my **dreams** in diaries, and I made lists of what I imagined my life would be like when I got older. When I look back on those early writings (yes, I still have my old diaries, lists, and journals), I feel an overwhelming sensation of deja vu, as if I was, at that time, writing about my future husband, my future life, my future kids, my future home, and my future career. My imagination was a template for my own story even as I was manifesting it into reality. The accuracy is uncanny, and I shiver in the most positive way to realize what a powerful tool a vivid imagination can be.

The idea of visualization is not just mere play, and it should not be reserved for use only with children. To me, imagination is an art and a tool. It's a type of visual, joyful meditation. It's manifestation and creative visualization. It's dreaming up and immersing yourself into fantastical worlds alongside characters with whom you empathize. You know—the kind of people you would like to meet, and experiences you would like to have. A vivid imagination is a gift that can provide a form of relaxation or a break from the seriousness of the day.

A vivid imagination is a crucial aspect of aspirational dreaming. In his groundbreaking book *Out of Our Minds: Learning to Be Creative*, Sir Ken Robinson writes, "Our world is the product of the ideas, beliefs and values of human imagination and culture that have shaped it over centuries. It has been created out of our minds as much as from the natural environment. The human mind is profoundly and uniquely creative, but too many people have no sense of their true talents." He's right. There is a direct line from creativity to imagination and innovation. Where imagination tells a story, creativity makes imagination possible. Innovation uses imagination and creativity to improve on what exists today.

Innovation takes an infinite number of forms. Our most famous inventors had vivid imaginations to create what never existed. Albert Einstein imagined a world lit by the marvel of electricity. Steve Jobs imagined a computer that was small enough to sit on your lap. Sure, not all of us will create something the world has never seen before. However, we can all be innovative in how we live our lives, create a home, raise our families, maintain friendships, and perform our professional responsibilities. Getting good at tapping into our imagination will help optimize whatever time we have here on earth.

Of all the dreams we can aim for, the biggest and most important is the dream of living lives that are happy and fulfilled. But all too often, we get caught up in just getting by day after day and we stop dreaming, innovating, and creating. What happens then? Well, we take our infinite potential, and we make it drab and boring.

Think of imagination as a muscle that needs to be exercised to make it stronger. This is why I love TV shows that emphasize the importance of imaginative thinking. Children are powered by intrinsically active imaginations that foster a feeling of freedom that lets them go with the flow. Most kids are open to new ideas, including the outlandish ones that sprout inside their minds. It's one of the saddest things about life that we get so caught up in the realities of existence—food, shelter, clothing—that we throw dreams and creativity overboard.

Think of imagination as a muscle that needs to be exercised to make it stronger.

If you find yourself feeling unmotivated and a little blah, strike a match to the imagination so that you can use it to take you to a place you want to go.

IMAGINING YOUR LIFE IN REAL LIFE

TRY THE POWER OF THE PINK BUBBLE:

To begin, sit in a quiet space and visualize one single moment in time that you imagine in your mind. Imagine a positive moment, something good that you really want to happen. Sit with that image in your mind for a little while as the details become clear and vivid. As you create your scene, start to envision the details: where you are, what you see, what you are saying, and how you are feeling. Play the scene in your mind over and over as a little movie, until it becomes so real you could almost touch it. Then, slowly, imagine a big pink bubble gum bubble. You can see the bubble come into your mind and you watch it grow bigger and bigger around your little movie. The translucence of the bubble enables you to see your visualization. Sit with that image of your scene inside a pink bubble for a moment. Then, when you are ready, release the pink bubble into the universe. In your mind, watch the bubble float away from you as it rises higher and higher into the sky and further and further into the distance. Wish it well on its journey. Then open your eyes and watch for signs that your visualization has become a reality. It may take minutes, or days, or months, and sometimes even years. But when you arrive at your visualization moment for real, you will experience a dizzying recognition. What you visualized in your imagination has been manifested.

One of my favorite memories is the visualization I did when I was pregnant with my first daughter. As is any mom-to-be, I was nervous and wanted more than anything to ensure that the baby would be healthy and safe. So I envisioned a specific, simple moment of happiness. It looked like this: I was holding my newborn, swaddled in a pink blanket. I was sitting on the edge of the bed, smiling down at the baby. My husband was next to me on the left, and my mother was next to me on the right. In this moment, we were all gazing at Hope, my new baby, as she slept contentedly in my arms. Then they both lovingly squeezed my shoulders at the same time. I smiled. The aura in the room exuded happiness, joy, wonder, serenity, and gratitude for this healthy, beautiful, amazing new life. This is what I wanted to happen. This is what I imagined. This is what I visualized. And just like in a movie, that small moment came to fruition, exactly how I imagined it would be.

PLAY WITH YOUR IMAGINATION:

After finishing a captivating book or movie, indulge in the power of your imagination. Contemplate how you would alter the ending. What changes would you make? Envision the ending you would have preferred. This exercise will ignite your creative thinking. Personally, I often find myself imagining the post-"happily ever after" lives of my beloved characters. For instance, I pictured Cinderella launching a shoe store inspired by her iconic glass slippers. I envisioned Prince Charming seeking therapy to grow beyond his charm. Even with my all-time favorite TV show, *Friends*, I imagined Monica and Chandler enjoying their life in Westchester, New York, and discovering a house on their block for Ross and Rachel to settle in when they are not in Paris for Rachel's work. They would continue their close-knit friendship, dropping by each other's homes or hanging out together, navigating the complexities of work-life balance, just like many of us do, but now with their children.

MAKE AN IMAGINATION LIST:

Throughout the day, we compile lists for various pur-poses—tasks to complete, groceries to buy, people to call back. Now, I invite you to create an imagina-tion and wish-fulfillment list. Dream of going on a vacation? Envision it vividly. Where would you like to go? Compose a list: —A warm destination. —A place where you can leisurely float in the turquoise blue sea. —A location reachable within a few hours. Is it your desire to reside in a neighborhood where everyone knows your name? Are you seeking a promotion at work? Longing to find a life partner? Jot it down. Craft a list that is specific and clear, even incorporating whimsical details. The more precise you are, the more your imagination will soar, and the greater the likeli-hood that the universe will guide you toward fulfilling your desires. Personally, I have always believed that my imagination has been my savior. It provided an escape as a child, and continues to bring immense joy to my life as an adult, allowing me to earn a living by conjur-ing up tales of talking tigers and blue puppies.

Do Nothing, Together

**Each person deserves a day away
in which no problems are confronted,
no solutions searched for.
Each of us needs to withdraw from the cares
which will not withdraw from us.**

—MAYA ANGELOU

I'm a big proponent of recharging myself. I know when I can keep going and I know when I need a pajama day. As an adult, I learned that a lot can be gleaned from a simple day of rest. For my family, it's a day of bonding, baking, and cooking together, watching *Gilmore Girls*, laughing, and me beating them at the card game Spit. (I'm the reigning champion; ask my sister, Jenn.) After a long week of work, homework, and meetings, everybody needs to use the weekend to just be. I find that after one of these days my mental gas tank is fueled up and my happiness quotient is fulfilled. New ideas are already churning, and I'm ready to take on another week.

Emotional exhaustion is real. Therapist Madeline Lucas, LCSW, says, "Emotional exhaustion is a state of feeling drained and burnt out: mentally, physically, and emotionally. This burnout happens as a result of living with ongoing stressors in one's life, whether at work, personal, social, etc." Before we let emotional exhaustion set in, we can practice self-care to keep it at bay. Laying low in a supportive environment with your favorite people will recharge your emotional energy. Setting your own pace to rest, eat mindfully, play, and exercise can ward off the most serious level of emotional exhaustion.

My favorite recharge philosophy is the Danish concept of hygge. Hygge, pronounced "hyoo-gah," sounds a bit like a character from a toddler's imagination or children's television program, which may account for why I love it so much. Hygge means creating a warm atmosphere and enjoying the good things in life with good people. Lighting candles is hygge. Snuggling under a soft blanket to rewatch a favorite movie for the zillionth time is hygge. Sitting around with family and friends, talking and laughing, imparts a feeling of coziness, comfort, and contentment that is the epitome of hygge.

Fitting time for family and friends into your schedule can seem more like yet another to-do item. Let's face it—there **are** always a million reasons not to do something. But you know how, when the going gets tough, everyone pulls together to get the job done? Same thing when it comes to carving out time to be together; everyone is rewarded when you do. Make up your collective mind that this will happen, and then do it! The point is to get together for happy reasons—or for no reason at all, because that works, too. Don't wait for the weddings and funerals. It's the stuff in between that makes life memorable. Call your friend who is also juggling a demanding schedule and plan something like doing your grocery shopping together. You can get a lot of catching up done going up and down the aisles. There will probably be at least one section where you'll collapse with laughter. (I'm betting on the cereal aisle.) You might even have time afterward for a cup of coffee at the in-store café. I swear to you: I once booked a mammogram with my friend who is a radiologist, just so we could have a whole hour to connect. (And who better to be with in case something went south?)

At first, taking time to do nothing might seem weird. We are programmed to expect a lot out of ourselves all day, every day. But you will find that incorporating time to do nothing is actually doing something. The key is to do nothing *intentionally*. Bring the respectful posture of being fully present to this downtime. Turn off the ringers and put the cell phones in a basket. Somewhere along the way, time devoted to doing nothing was sacrificed, and we need to get it back into our lives.

Preschoolers thrive when they are given alone time during which they can lose themselves in coloring or imaginative play with dolls and blocks. These quiet intervals give them time to puzzle over and figure things out. Adults need solo space, too. Time spent in this way is analogous

> We are programmed to expect a lot out of ourselves all day, every day. But you will find that incorporating time to do nothing is actually doing something. The key is to do nothing intentionally.

to conscious breathing. It's like taking deep breaths with your brain. Give yourself a gift by setting aside time to do something important—by doing nothing.

DOING NOTHING IN REAL LIFE

HAVE YOUR OWN PAJAMA DAY:

Literally, don't get out of your coziest pjs—and don't feel bad about it. Some of my best days are when the four of us in my family chill out and do nothing. Pajama Day is the day to relax, make some tea, wear a moisturizing mask, take a bath, or snuggle up to watch TV. Whatever brings you joy, do. Whatever doesn't bring you joy, leave for tomorrow, if you can. Having your own Pajama Day is a gift to yourself.

TURN OFF SOCIAL MEDIA:

I have a friend who takes a social media break every August. It's lovely. She takes that time to be in the moment, not documenting her life or scrolling through other's lives. She believes that this break is a "sharpening of her saw" before September rolls around and we're off to the races again. I have bought into this amazing idea and have followed suit. It feels good!

TAKE A DRIVE TO NOWHERE:

In every area of my life, I have always had a destination.
The idea of taking a drive or a walk with no destination
was new to me. My husband loves to do this. It's his
version of doing nothing. Taking a destination-free
drive with him has brought us to some beautiful places.
We sing along the way, stopping wherever and whenever we want. We turn up the radio, share stories,
and laugh. Being free of time and place has helped us
reconnect.

Laugh, Every Day

**Trouble knocked at the door,
but, hearing laughter, hurried away.**

—BENJAMIN FRANKLIN

I remember the first time I made my mother laugh. I remember it well because I felt powerful and seen, and I loved seeing her so happy. I was seven years old, and my sister was four. We were riding in the back of the family car, with my parents in the front. We were going to my grandparents' house, which always seemed to make my parents angsty. As the conversation in the front seat got louder and more stressed, I sank into the back seat and worried. Then an idea came to me. I looked at my shoes and my white frilly socks; yep, this would do. I took them off. I popped the white socks over my hands and launched a dialogue between the two sock puppets. They talked to each other and told silly jokes. My sister started giggling. Then she laughed so hard she got the hiccups. The turning point came when my mother, whose eyes were glistening with tears by this point in the conversation with my father, glanced back and asked, "Angela, what are you doing?"

And then she laughed. She laughed and laughed at my silly sock puppets.

The tension in the car disappeared. Even my father, who was quite stoic, had to chuckle. My mom made a comment that I've never forgotten. She said that I was "so creative." My heart glowed with the unexpected praise.

Was this the first time I realized the power of humor? Maybe. What I know for sure is that laughter chased trouble out of town, even if only for a little while.

Humor is the secret sauce for bonding with people of all ages. The science behind the many benefits of humor has guided me in writing preschool humor into my shows. I use humor to form emotional bonds between our viewers and our characters, as well as to take the stress out of emotional situations. Most importantly, I've strived to make sure that my shows help kids flex their humor muscles so that they'll appreciate the value of using humor for the rest of their lives.

Why do we adults seem to have lost our sense of humor? We need to laugh at ourselves, and we need to laugh with others. The crucial thing to remember is that we should never laugh *at* others, but *with* others. We also need to get better at being self-deprecating when it is appropriate. If you can laugh at yourself, then you open the window, so to speak, and others are able to laugh along with you.

Humor is the secret sauce for bonding with people of all ages.

The physical, emotional, and relational benefits to laughter have been well documented. According to CNN correspondent Katie Hunt, hundreds of years ago, "Laughter was the glue that kept the group together. The idea was that laughter was an external signal that can tell the group everything is OK, we can relax. The belief is that, over the centuries, the brain kept these connections so that we now laugh when we hear things that are relaxing, funny, surprising, and amusing." Similarly, a study done by Robert Levenson at the University of California, Berkeley, suggests that laughter is the glue that keeps romantic relationships together. Satisfied couples laugh more than unsatisfied ones. There is a reason laughter is considered the "best medicine." The physical act of laughing delivers pleasure-inducing dopamine and boosts endorphins, similar to what happens during an intense workout. According to the Mayo Clinic, a good laugh has both short- and long-term benefits. Laughter enhances the intake of oxygen-rich air, decreases stress, beefs up immune responses, boosts memory levels, lowers cortisol levels, protects against heart disease, and eradicates pent-up tension.

Humor is a top-notch bonding tool. When we laugh together, we're sharing a mutual experience that connects us in ways few other experiences can. As Maya Angelou put it, "At the end of the day people won't remember what you said or did, they will remember how you made them feel." And joy is something we all want to feel, right?

Whether you're alone or with your best friend, coworkers, or children, it is **important** you laugh every single day. What we're going for here is not just a chuckle or guffaw but a big belly laugh. Preschool humor works for grown-ups, too, so don't underestimate the power of a booty dance to get the endorphins flowing.

FINDING THE LAUGHTER IN REAL LIFE

LAUGHTER AS RESUSCITATION:

Like CPR, laughter will breathe new life into your attitude, your outlook, your situation. Humor is my go-to strategy for dealing with conflict, my children, my husband, and my work life. I like to say that diffusing with humor is the "snack" of strategies: it's always good to have on hand, and you never know when you're going to need it. At Thanksgiving dinner, someone said something stressful about the state of the world. My response was to sing "We Are the World," (note: I cannot sing) and everyone joined in. Silly? Guilty as charged. But it worked; it broke the tension. Everyone took a breath, and we went on from there.

LAUGHTER AS RECALIBRATION:

For better or worse, your mood is up to you. While you cannot control the way other people speak, act, or move about the world, one thing is constant: You can decide how to react to what they do. So even if you are feeling the furthest thing from belly laughter, remember that you attract what you put out into the world. Feelings happen. Serious challenges happen, too. But it is when life and heavy emotions make laughter and joy seem most impossible that laughter and joy are most needed.

Ask yourself, "How badly do I want to feel good?" Okay. Recalibrate. You have the agency to make it happen.

LAUGHTER AS RECOGNITION:

When we can laugh at ourselves, we are setting the stage for self-awareness that facilitates relationships. There's a big difference between *being* the joke and *being in on* the joke. If we have enough self-recognition to see how we fit into this humorous situation, then we free ourselves and everybody else to enjoy a moment of shared bonding. We get it. We are not above it. This is a thing that happens to all of us, and right now, it just happens to be my turn.

Connection happens when we allow ourselves to be vulnerable—when we are able to recognize ourselves and the part we play in the comedy. There is nothing more human or relatable than adults laughing at themselves when they have done something stupid, embarrassing, or goofy. So go ahead and laugh— hard—at yourself!

LIFE CLUE #14

Create Your Own Neighborhood

The underlying message of the Neighborhood is that if somebody cares about you, it's possible that you'll care about others. 'You are special, and so is your neighbor'— that part is essential: that you're not the only special person in the world.

—FRED ROGERS

Because Fred Rogers respected children's intelligence, he often talked about difficult things that parents avoided discussing with their kids such as death and divorce. It seemed as though his "visits" were as important to him as they were to his young audience. He was there at the same time every day. All kids had to do was turn on the television. He was interesting, and he was interested in YOU. He was soft-spoken and patient, and he liked you just the way you were. He was happy you were his neighbor.

In my work, we meticulously design distinct types of neighborhoods, with an aim to crafting a space where young ones feel safe, secure, and at ease—a neighborhood where everyone recognizes you and greets you with a smile. These are communities rich in diversity, where varied families coexist harmoniously. In *Daniel Tiger's Neighborhood*, we introduced Henrietta Pussycat as a single mother and Uncle X the Owl as the guardian of his nephew O. We showcased loving families of different shapes, sizes, and hues. We depicted neighbors who might have differing views but still listen to and learn from one another.

> *Taking an active role in your neighborhood will bring you joy and help you make the most of every moment.*

While I understand that this is an imaginary, animated world and not an actual representation of everyday life, it mirrors the world as seen through the inquisitive, creative, and playful eyes of many preschoolers. These qualities are what many seek as they age and confront life's realities. I firmly believe that for children aged 0–5, we can maintain this enchanting "neighborhood" bubble, gradually introducing them to the broader world so they can approach its truths with enduring optimism. Where you live and work, and the family you belong to, is your neighborhood. When you make your life your neighborhood, you are better able to see yourself as a neighbor or colleague, a daughter or son, a sister or brother, and a mentor or friend. Taking an active role in your neighborhood will bring you joy and help you make the most of every moment. You'll have a fresh appreciation for what it means to demonstrate kindness with a smile, to help out in small ways, to be fully present and thoughtful. You will realize how much you are missed when you are not there.

It's true that we don't live in a place like *Daniel Tiger's Neighborhood*, or Stars Hollow of *Gilmore Girls*, where everyone knows your name and conflicts are resolved quickly and beautifully. My personal dream would be to live inside a musical where people sing my theme song when I walk down the street. Until that day comes, we can make sure that what we put out into our neighborhood is what we want coming back to us. When we think of ourselves as a little tiger cub in our space, we realize that we are Daniel, living in our own neighborhood. It's up to us to write the script of our lives.

YOUR NEIGHBORHOOD IN REAL LIFE

THE POWER OF KNOWING THE BASICS:

Basic premise #1 is that you are the creator of your neighborhood. Basic premise #2 is that what you exude will determine what your neighborhood is. In other words, if you want something good from your neighborhood, you've got to put good things into it. What does this look like in real life? Well, start with "Hello" and "Good morning." When you start there, you're communicating the message "I see you." Then reach into your bag of LIFE CLUES and listen attentively by taking a moment. Breathe. Listen in order to understand. Now you're communicating "I hear you." Basic premise #3 is discovering what you truly care about, and what you can learn from the people in your neighborhood.

THE POWER OF GRATITUDE:

As you make your life richer, think about all the people who give you reasons to smile, and then go out of your way to thank them. What about the coworker who always compliments you after your presentation? What about the barista who knows your order before you've even said good morning, or the grocery store clerk who knows that you love fresh tomatoes? Thinking about the people in the neighborhood who make you smile will make the daily scenes in your life unfold like a richly illustrated storybook.

For this reason, I've penned numerous episodes centered on gratitude, kindness, and empathy for children. In one of my favorites, the "Thankful Day" episode of *Daniel Tiger*, we introduced a "thankful tree." Neighbors penned notes expressing their gratitude—Daniel expressed thanks for Grandpere's visit, while Mom was thankful for the banana bread Baker Aker makes for her each year. These notes were then displayed on a tree in the Enchanted Garden for everyone to see. The community gathers around the tree, reading the sentiments aloud. This concept resonated with me personally. For Thanksgiving, I introduced my own version of the "Thankful Tree" (a quaint plant from

Trader Joe's) to my extended family. We all wrote and hung our notes of gratitude. While it might seem a bit cheesy at the outset, the moment became deeply touching, especially when the older generation—like my mom and grandmother—recognized how much they are cherished.

In helping others feel seen, we ourselves are rewarded by feeling more visible. When we open our hearts to the idea that if this one person were not here tomorrow, there would be a terrible void in the neighborhood, we realize that he or she would be missed. This kind of awareness reverberates. We can appreciate the fact that if we weren't there, we would be sorely missed, too. Carrying around that kind of sensitivity makes life sparkle. When we live with grateful hearts, we see that everyone is precious, every day is priceless, and every interaction is an opportunity to do good.

THE POWER OF THE KINDNESS LOOP:

Celebrating what each person gives to you, and what you give to him or her, is part of a kindness loop. Finding at least one good thing in every person and going out of your way to be kind will come back to you in spades. According to Steve Siegle, writing for the Mayo Clinic on "The Art of Kindness," "Kindness has been shown to increase self-esteem, empathy and compassion, and improve mood. It can decrease blood pressure and cortisol, a stress hormone, which directly impacts stress levels. People who give of themselves in a balanced way also tend to be healthier and live longer. **So** kindness can increase your sense of connectivity with others, which can directly impact loneliness, improve low mood and enhance relationships in general. It also can be contagious." So hop on the Trolley with O the Owl, sing and dance to your own theme song, and aim a smile at everyone you see on your way home. Doing so will brighten everyone's day, including yours.

Be Like Daniel Tiger and Buddy Up

I've got magic beans.

—RACHEL on the TV show _Friends_

Sometimes the biggest blessings in life are right in front of you—or sitting at the next table. As a surprise, a friend of mine sat me at the head table in a ceremony where Mister Rogers was being honored. This was a nail-biting, heart-fluttering moment! What if Mister Rogers wasn't the friend I had thought he was through the television set?

I felt as though I was in that first big executive meeting all over again. I turned into an observer. Throughout the entire meal, I sat and stared. I watched as his kind smile and gentle words worked their magic on each person he talked to. His laugh came easily, and he shared personal stories with a generosity we don't see very often. At last, he glanced my way, tilted his head, and said, "I don't think we've met. I'm Fred."

I shook his outstretched hand as steadily as I could, given the fact that I was trembling. Awkwardly, I was too emotional to introduce myself. My colleagues jumped in to introduce me. "Fred, she created the newest hit show, *Blue's Clues*." His eyes sparkled with recognition. I then told him something that I had been wanting to tell him for years: "*You* are the reason I went into children's television. If I can reach one kid the way you reached me, I will be very happy."

He paused. (*He took a moment! LIFE CLUE #2!!*)

"What is your name?" he asked. I laughed and told him.

And then he said words that will forever remain in my heart and soul.

"*Blue's Clues* is one of the only shows for children I like right now," he said. "I see all the hard work and child development theory in it. I am just so proud of you."

I'm not ashamed to say that I cried. Like, two tears trickled down my face. MISTER ROGERS WAS PROUD OF ME! And then, just as my head was exploding, Fred hugged me. I had that beautiful, full-circle moment where I got to hug my friend, the person who started our friendship through the television. Fred invited me to Pittsburgh to watch him shoot an episode of *Mister Rogers' Neighborhood*. I smiled through my tears and accepted his invitation. I was on a plane the next week, and we were real-life friends from that day on.

Friends of all kinds—be they real, imaginary, next door, or on TV—are important. Just as countless people have impacted who you are as a person, you have had an impact on countless others.

The manner in which we craft character in children's television is paramount. These characters are more than mere figures on a screen; they're trusted friends. They aren't just on your TV—they join play dates in your living room, accompany you on car rides, and sometimes even take a virtual seat at your family dinner table. To the children who adore them, our characters are tangible, living entities. They're buddies. My little nephew, for instance, eagerly shares his drawings and engages in lively chats with Daniel Tiger whenever Daniel appears on the screen. To him, Daniel is a genuine friend.

Much like the meticulous neighborhoods we design, we invest deep thought—encompassing appearance, dialogue, attire, mannerisms, and defining personality traits—into the formation of our characters. Our intention is to imbue them with qualities that research indicates are crucial for the holistic growth of children. Take Daniel Tiger, for example: he mirrors a three-year-old who is kind-hearted and bountiful, yet occasionally struggles with sharing or yearning for undivided parental attention. While Daniel confronts typical preschool challenges, he simultaneously stands as a commendable role model. Real children often emulate him, whether it's trying a novel food, remembering to use the bathroom, or practicing polite behaviors like saying "please" and "thank you."

With *Blue's Clues*, I approached the characters of Steve, Joe, and Josh differently than I did Daniel. They serve as trusted guides, akin to resourceful and fun camp counselors, mentors of friendship. This choice aims to make young viewers feel emboldened and cherished by the relationship. The essence of Steve, Joe, and Josh, while individually unique, is rooted in the profound impact that attentive listening, validation, and genuine care can have on a young mind.

I believe it's essential to depict an array of positive friendships in our programs because this lays a solid foundation for real-world relationships as children grow.

Of course making friends and being friends with others takes work and commitment, especially when we live busy, sometimes over-scheduled lives. What is essential is that you have at least one special person you know you can lean on, someone who is there for you whenever you need a shoulder, an ear, or a new perspective.

It's clear that friends *enrich* our lives. But research shows that having the right people to trust and rely on can actually *lengthen* your life. According to *Captivate: The Science of Succeeding with People* by Vanessa Van Edwards, friendships are as important to our overall well-being as diet and exercise.

More specifically, according to the Mayo Clinic, having a good friend is linked to physiologically measurable indicators of good health,

What is essential is that you have at least one special person you know you can lean on, someone who is there for you whenever you need a shoulder, an ear, or a new perspective.

including lower blood pressure, lower body mass index, reduced inflammation, and fewer risks for diabetes. In another study, researchers found that the people who maintained active friendships of the highest quality are less likely to get sick if they are exposed to a common cold. Good friends boost our immunity.

Just as our TV characters depict friends who are on their side, we need a supportive sidekick in real life, too. Daniel Tiger has O the Owl; Miss Elaina has Katerina Kittycat; and Josh has Blue. Friends are the backbone of our lives, but we can and should have a variety of friends—people who tick different boxes— because one person cannot be everything to someone else. Different people can be better in different situations; one friend may offer insight, another, encouragement. There's the friend you can call when things are going poorly and the friend you call when you want to have fun. If you have someone in your life who is the same person in all categories, that is wonderful (and I want their cell number). If not, then each of the other friends taken individually adds up to the same high quality.

When my daughters were in middle school, I talked to them about the idea that not all best girlfriends look or act like the characters in the sitcom *Friends*. As much as we want to sit on the couch in Central Perk Cafe with our friends, people in real life aren't as well-scripted as they are on television. Good friendships take work, and not everyone is up to the kind of work it takes to maintain a close friendship. As you choose your friends, remember these three things: First, look for the best in everyone. Second, be mindful that you can rely on different friends for different things, which means that you won't have to put so much pressure on one singular relationship. And third, remember that the best way to **find** a friend is to be a friend to someone else.

FRIENDSHIP IN REAL LIFE

BE OBSERVANT AND KIND:

Take the time to observe and appreciate the qualities and actions of those around you. Look for the best in everyone and practice kindness in your interactions. This doesn't mean you'll become friends with everyone you meet, but when we honor those around us, we are living from a place of compassion and understanding, which are key components to happiness and joy.

BE A GOOD FRIEND:

The best way to have strong friendships is to be mindful of your relationships. Focus on being a supportive and reliable friend to others. Spend time together. Offer a shoulder to lean on, lend a listening ear, and provide a fresh perspective when needed. Show up for your friends and be there for them when they need you. What we give to others is often what we receive back.

HOLD ON TO YOUR SISTER (OR BROTHER, OR COUSIN):

Believe me, if you are lucky enough to have a sister, hold on to her. Who else knows your innermost secrets of growing up, or what the roots of your hair actually look like? Who is at your side—and on your side—for all the family drama? So much history, so many similarities, and so many differences. I enjoy my sister for who she is, and how much she adds to my life. She makes my life a whole lot richer. Family members can be friends, too. Sometimes your best friends.

Ugga Mugga

**Surround yourself with only people
who are going to lift you higher.**

—OPRAH WINFREY

"Ugga Mugga" means "I love you."

In *Mister Rogers' Neighborhood*, Daniel Tiger said "Ugga Mugga" as his love phrase. Although this might be recalled only by superfans, I knew I wanted to include it in the vernacular of *Daniel Tiger's Neighborhood*. I wanted kids everywhere to feel the (almost) inexpressible love that Daniel had for his family, friends, neighbors, and the kids who were watching. And so, at the end of every episode, Daniel embraces the camera with his little paws on either side, gives a "nose nuzzle" to the children who are watching, and says, "Ugga Mugga." It's beautiful.

Surrounding yourself with people who lift you up, value you, and make you feel deeply loved is the most important emotional blessing we can give ourselves. It's so important that we want to impart this idealogy to our kids from the start. Kids know this instinctively. When kids love something, they love it with their whole body, heart, and soul. They are loyal to that loved one—whether it's you, first and foremost, or a blankie, a stuffed toy, or a pet turtle in a tank—forever.

The first time I looked into the eyes of my newborn daughters, I felt an overpowering surge of emotion, as if the wind had been sucked out of me. It was love at first sight, which is to say that the deep feeling of agape wasn't there—not quite yet. My eldest daughter had eyes so wide, she looked like a little old lady with the wisdom of the world. I smiled, introduced myself as her mommy, and told her that her name was Hope. She clasped her hands in front of herself, as if she was thinking about all of this. She didn't leave our strong gaze until she drifted off to sleep in my arms. My second daughter came out screaming. She was comfortable where she was, thank you very much. Enduring a C-section birth, I imagine, would feel like the rudest awakening. She screamed until they put her in my arms, but stopped mid-scream when she heard my voice. Her little mouth made that cute O shape as if she was thinking, "Oh, that's why I'm here. It's you!"

I cried and told her that I was her mom and that her name was Ella. She stared deeply into my eyes, and—I kid you not—she smiled and fell asleep. I was a goner.

Being in love with my girls has been the highlight of my life. My husband and I marvel at the individuals they have grown into. Truth be told, they are the same people who came out of the womb: fiery, headstrong, reflective, analytical, and loving.

I've spent my whole life either around kids or studying kids. I feel a tremendous responsibility to my kids and to everybody else's kids. To me, children are hearts that have arms and legs—all they want is to be loved.

Children, especially preschoolers, show you how they feel in full force. If they are sad, you know it from the adorable pouty face. If they are mad, you know it by the meltdowns or the stomping feet. If they are feeling love, they will run at you full steam to wrap you in their best hugs. Preschoolers are the real deal. They wear their emotions on their sleeves, and we adults could learn a thing or two from this enviable trait. Adults don't show our love as readily as children. We don't hug hard anymore. Maybe it's because we're afraid that someone may not love hard in return, and so we hold back.

Love is a vulnerable act. Researcher and author Brené Brown defines vulnerability as "uncertainty, risk, and emotional exposure." It's that unstable feeling we get when we step out of our comfort zone or do something that forces us to give up the feeling that we're in control. Still, Brown argues that we need to be vulnerable, as it is "the birthplace for joy, creativity, authenticity, and love." With vulnerability, we can let our guard down and be seen for who we are. Vulnerability is a strength, not a weakness.

Love is a vulnerable act.

Vulnerability allows us to open up about how we feel, and the gift it imparts is that it helps us feel connected.

Science supports the theory that people who had warm, affectionate parents in childhood go on to live better lives. According to a Harvard study published in *Social Science & Medicine*, "people who remember their parents as warm and loving are flourishing at much higher rates in adulthood, such as happiness, self-acceptance, social relationships, and being more likely to contribute to the community." The inverse is true as well. Adults who were disciplined harshly were "more likely to suffer from anxiety, depression, or addiction." Adults who were overprotected as children also "struggled with chronic anxiety and poor self-image because their parents kept them from opportunities to grow coping skills." The bottom line is that love for our children, and the way we demonstrate and express that love, makes a difference.

As a creator for children's television, I take this responsibility to heart. Characters on my shows are expressions of love and care. They bond with viewers through the "interactive" way they look through the camera and invite the kids into their neighborhoods. Daniel Tiger, all of his friends, and Blue and all of her friends lean in and want the kids at home to play with them, care about them, solve problems with them, and celebrate with them. In the end, they are more than friends; they are true embodiments of love. Daniel says "Ugga Mugga," Blue gives a screen-licking kiss, and Steve, Joe, and Josh commend the kids at home for their effort and hard work. Super Why and the Super Readers join hands in a circle with the home viewer's hand and celebrate at the end of every show with a "Hip Hip Hooray!" It's all designed to reinforce the importance of love and connection.

I am telling you right now: Please, with their permission, hug **your** child, your partner, your friends. If you are lucky enough to have parents and grandparents in your life, hug them, too. Better yet, write them a letter and tell them how you feel. How many times have we heard loving thoughts expressed after someone is out of the room, or, worse still, after he or she has passed on?

Of course, I wouldn't suggest that you hug your colleague at work or strangers on the street. But show them a little love. Compliment them, talk about something they love, and make sure they know you care. We want to bestow on as many people as we can the feeling of a hug or an Ugga Mugga. The positive feelings you give come right back to you as an extra little bonus.

It's no secret that I'm as mushy-gushy as they come. I strongly believe that the more love you put out into the world, the more love you will get back. I stand by my philosophy that if you live from an intentional place of love, your world will explode with beauty.

UGGA MUGGA IN THE REAL WORLD

THE POWER OF LOVING HARD:

Passion has always been one of the driving forces in my life. Passion is what I feel when I know I'm loving something or someone hard. Passion is worth finding, cultivating, and fighting for. Loving hard is that beautiful, passionate kiss with our partners that we all deserve. It's driving your kids a long distance to something that is important to them. It's the joy in sharing a new Brené Brown or Glennon Doyle podcast with your friends. To me, finding something that I love deeply has been the North Star in my life. Whether you love playing the piano or painting or cooking, love it hard and with passion—and feel the joy.

THE POWER OF LETTING YOURSELF BE LOVED HARD:

Sometimes it's hard to let *yourself* be loved hard. How do we do that? And why do we do that?!

We start with being vulnerable. We have to admit to ourselves—and to the universe—how much we want and need to be loved. I know it feels like putting yourself out on a ledge by proclaiming to the world that you need another person. It's not easy, and it may take a lot of effort to open up completely. But when you take these calculated risks of letting go and trusting, you will feel the power of your own vulnerability. For me, letting myself be loved hard was scary at first. But now it's my anchor, and it truly allows me to stand up straight and take more calculated risks in my work and life. It's the beautiful, scary aspects of life that become the most memorable.

THE POWER OF TELLING PEOPLE YOU LOVE THEM:

I'm not sure why there are absolutely beautiful eulogies at funerals, but seldom the mushy, gushy toasts when our loved ones are alive. A few years ago, I used my commute on the Metro-North line to write letters to people near and dear to me to tell them how I feel about them and why. I tried to be specific when writing about my feelings, and how much these people had touched me throughout my life. Some of my friends still carry my letters around with them in their wallets. When they are feeling low, they reread them. It makes me so happy every time I hear that!

Don't Say Fun–Be Fun

**Always work hard and have fun in
what you do because I think that's when you're
more successful. You have to choose to do it.**

—SIMONE BILES

When I worked at Nickelodeon, Geraldine Laybourne, the visionary president of the network, believed in putting kids at the center of everything we do. Nickelodeon's philosophy started with the idea that kids don't want to be told what to think. Kids don't want to be told whether something is funny. So the adage of "Don't say fun—be fun" was born. We lived by that motto at Nickelodeon, and I believe it is as relevant today as it was then. As Gerry put it, "I wouldn't allow any of our producers to say 'fun' on the air. If they wanted to show kids that we were fun and funny, they had to be it." In other words, put action before words. If you love someone, show it with how you act toward that person. If something is innovative, show us how and why, don't just proclaim it. If something is funny, be funny. Make me laugh.

For some reason, fun is often an afterthought for adults. How many times have we put off doing something fun until we have gotten through the daily tasks we need to do? Just like when it comes to self-care, we too often deprioritize what makes us happy. We need to readjust, reevaluate, and rediscover which things should come first.

As children's television writers, we sometimes brainstorm the most ridiculous things. Like talking salt and pepper shakers who get married and have a condiment family, or a side table drawer who is excited to play Blue's Clues, but too shy to sing in the Backyard Musical. We love our work so much that sometimes we burst out in fits of laughter over one storyline or another. I remember a colleague walking by the conference room and stating, "I can't imagine that work is happening in this room. There is way too much fun going on in there." Sorry to disappoint. Work was, in fact, happening, and yes, there was *also* way too much fun. We ended up winning an Emmy for that season's work on *Daniel Tiger's Neighborhood*. I believe that the love and fun shone right through the screen.

Unsurprisingly, there is a body of science behind fun. As Catherine Price, a *Science* journalist, put it, "We may be thinking about 'fun' entirely wrong." According to Price, we associate fun as being frivolous, lighthearted, and activity based. Often, we think of it as something meant for kids. But fun is actually a vital component of living a healthier, happier, fuller life. "The more often we experience it, the more we will feel like we're actually alive," she says. It's been proven that having fun as adults is critical. According to Michael Forman in an article for *Wanderlust*, having fun "releases endorphins, improves brain functionality, memory, stimulates creativity, and can help keep us young."

So how can we fit more fun into our lives?

> Just like when it comes to self-care, we too often deprioritize what makes us happy. We need to readjust, reevaluate, and rediscover which things should come first.

HAVING FUN IN REAL LIFE

CULTIVATE FUN:

I have a **passion** for laughter. It just makes us feel better. Think of what makes you laugh, get inspiration from your childhood or from TV shows or your own life experiences, and re-create them. When my girls were little, we made a game out of having to stop whatever we were doing when their favorite songs came on and dance together (in case you were wondering, the songs were Taylor Swift's "You Belong to Me" and "Bubbly" by Colbie Caillat). Sometimes we danced (and laughed) in the middle of a CVS store, but mostly we danced in our kitchen. Some days we played "pretend restaurant." Either my husband and I would be the chef and waitstaff and the girls would be our customers, or we would flip it. We have "dress up" dinners or "photo shoots" in the snow or at the park. (We would be the photographers.) Silly, I know, but that's the point.

At work, before delving into our meetings, we'd take a moment to share laughs about our personal lives. Play-Doh and Slime were always at the ready to fuel our brainstorming sessions. We hosted Halloween dress-up parties in the conference room (or on Zoom) and we initiated a "Kindness Secret Elf" tradition, drawing names and performing thoughtful gestures for that person throughout the month of December.

TRACK YOUR FUN:

I am 100 percent that person who gets excited when my circles complete on my Apple watch. Similarly, I think we should track and take note of our moments of fun. What if we wrote things on little slips of paper that made us laugh and then put them in a mason jar? Like the time we tried to use sparklers in the rain on the Fourth of July, or the time we did a meatball-eating contest with my big Italian family (my mom won!)? When we feel sad, we reach into the mason jar and read a few of them. Taking it a step further, what if we filled our calendar with a fun activity every day? Something small and maybe a little silly? Here's an idea: For Monday at 3 p.m., write, "Play music loudly." For Tuesday at 6 p.m., write, "Make tacos for Taco Tuesday." What about making a heart-shaped pizza for no reason, or having pancakes for dinner? Or our favorite: Create a "family game" with questions from different categories to see who knows one another best.

TALK FUN:

At dinnertime, instead of asking, "How was your day" or "Tell me something you learned," ask what made each person laugh. Laugh together, talk about the absurd and beautiful parts of the day, swap stories, and inspire one another.

Be Present

**Wherever you are, be there totally.
If you find your here and now intolerable and
it makes you unhappy, you have three options:
remove yourself from the situation, change it,
or accept it totally.**

—ECKHART TOLLE

We lost my mother to cancer at seventy-six years old. Though my mother and I didn't always see eye to eye, I was devastated by her loss. To make matters worse, it was heart-wrenching to watch her suffer during COVID. She wasn't able to be around her loved ones as much as she wanted, and she had to endure chemo infusions alone because we weren't allowed in during her treatments. This experience of love and loss taught me and my sister to live in the moment at all times.

My sister and I both remember where we were when we got the call about our mother's diagnosis. It was as if time stood still. We vowed to be as present with her as we could. Our families surrounded her with love, and we were physically there with her at the end. Nothing else mattered but providing her with good stories, her favorite music, and her favorite foods, even when she could eat only just a little bit. We vowed to take it one day at a time and be present with her until the end. We stayed true to our promises, and I believe that we got as much from that time as our mom did. Being together, all of us, with our cousin, our spouses, **and** our kids was a gift. We shared the hard parts with one another just as we shared the good parts. We had great conversations with our kids about life. We realized that we needed to be together more often to feed our souls, figure out how not to let stress beat us down, and enjoy the journey more than the destination. I finally understood what that saying meant, and I took it to heart from that day forward.

Active listening is a gift of time that you give to yourself and to another.

Being there for someone who was dying was a life lesson I will carry with me forever. Being present is a reciprocal process. It is actively listening to someone, staying in their story, and encouraging them to tell you more, all while being empathetic and nurturing. It's about reacting to someone else, nodding, asking questions, and elaborating on what they are saying. Active listening is the cornerstone of the interactive dialogue I have scripted for all my shows. Steve, Joe, Josh, and Daniel Tiger model active listening as they lean into the camera, nod, and pause after asking a question.

Active listening is not thinking about what you are going to say next. No phones. No scanning the room for the next person to talk to. Active listening is a gift of time that you give to yourself and to another. According to Michael Mathieu, CEO of BeAlive Media, "When you have a conversation with somebody, you're not going to get the nuances of the conversation if you're doing too many things. If somebody picks up the phone, stop your email, stop what you're doing, listen and have that conversation with the person and then move on. I try to be present so I can enjoy the richness and quality of interactions with people. Most people can't multitask without losing something in each of those tasks."

I wish I had known then what I know now because the following confrontation would never have happened.

We went on vacation when my daughters were eight and five. I was checking my email when my five-year-old, hands on hips, stomped over to me. She looked me right in the eye and said, "This is not a phone-cation, this is not an email-cation, this is a VA-CATION!" I took the hint. I put away my phone and remained present for the rest of the time we had together. Now that our girls are twenty-two and nineteen, I cry thinking about what could have possibly been more important than being with them and spending time with them exclusively.

Being present has many scientifically proven benefits. According to an article in *Virtuagym* (2020), studies have shown that being present helps "your focus, your concentration, your learning, your listening skills and your memory." Being present is also linked to a "decrease in stress and anxiety" because you are grounding yourself in the present moment versus focusing on the worries of the past or future.

The tightrope we need to walk is the balance between looking toward the future, ruminating on the past, and living in the present. With this kind of multi-layered focus, we will be able to better discern between what others feel is important to us and what we deeply know to actually be most important to us.

BEING PRESENT IN REAL LIFE

STUDY BODY LANGUAGE:

Be aware of the signals you are sending with your posture, your arms and hands, the tilt of your head, and the directness of your gaze. We have long been aware of the communicative significance of that first handshake. But we're not so schooled in how we handle our physical selves from the handshake to the goodbye, which is also important. Once you are better at reading body language and become more aware of how your body language is coming across to others, you will be better at listening actively.

PRACTICE DISCONNECTING FROM TECHNOLOGY:

The importance of disconnecting from technology cannot be overstated. Every once in a while, unplug yourself from your devices so you can feel what it's like to be in the present moment. Turn off the television, don't check your email, and don't answer the phone for a period of time every day. Take note of how you feel. Anxious? Jittery? Stay present as you move through these feelings. Don't be surprised if freedom and relief soon wash over you.

PRACTICE ACTIVE LISTENING:

And I mean practice. Practice as if there's going to be an Active Listening Recital and you are in deep trouble if you don't know this thing by heart. First, put away your phone. Clear away what's on your mind. Lean into the conversation. Nod, smile, let your face reflect appropriate reactions and emotions, but do not interrupt the flow of what the other person is saying. Don't cross your arms, scowl, or lean back—these are body language signals that are off-putting. Instead of allowing your mind to race toward what you might say when it's your turn to speak, try to stay in the moment with whatever the other person is talking about. Trust the process of being empathetic. You'll be better able to ask follow-up questions.

Always Say Goodbye

**Now it's time for so long,
but we'll sing just one more song.
Thanks for doing your part; you sure are smart.
With me and you and my dog Blue,
we can do anything that we wanna do.**

—BLUE'S CLUES

When I was a little girl, my mother thought it was better to slip away without saying goodbye. I remember being immersed in play and then frantically looking for her only to discover a babysitter, who would tell me that my mother had gone out to dinner, or—I kid you not—left for a week's vacation. Every time this happened, it stung. Like a low-grade fever, dread ran through me constantly.

Research in the field of child development talks a lot about respecting young children. Kids deserve respect for their point of view, their feelings, and their outlook on life. To say a proper goodbye to children, no matter what age, is to actively demonstrate respect. In essence, saying goodbye honors their existence. Is saying goodbye harder than slipping away and not dealing with the emotions of announcing your exit? Absolutely. Kids don't make it easy to leave them— after all, you represent security, and all they want is to be with you. But talking for a few minutes with your child about where you are going and when you'll be back is important. Heck, if nothing else, it's common courtesy.

On *Daniel Tiger's Neighborhood*, we sang the song "Grownups Come Back" for this exact reason. The assurance that you'll be back is all most kids need. The reason all my shows have closing songs like "Now It's Time for So Long" is to cue the kids that the show is coming to an end. Helping your child with transitions is one of the finest ways you can help him or her grow up. Getting better at making transitions nurtures the sense of self, fuels confidence, and increases willingness to give independence a try.

There is a body of research behind why it's important to nurture your child. What may surprise you is that there is also research to show why, as an adult, it is essential to nurture your inner child. A child's brain is especially receptive from birth until about age four, so baby and toddler experiences leave a big imprint. What we do and how we are treated will have a significant impact on our emotional well-being, the patterns and strategies we develop to cope with emotions, and the information we process about who we are as we go forward in life. Put another way, our brains create our own unique survival tactics. These tactics were informed by the

> There is a body of research behind why it's important to nurture your child. What may surprise you is that there is also research to show why, as an adult, it is essential to nurture your inner child.

adults in our lives through our observations of how they processed emotions, particularly sadness and anger. Our tactics are also shaped by how we were treated by the adults in our lives. What we see and how we are loved becomes a sort of go-to script for the unconscious mind. Saying goodbye is a small way to ensure that our child (and his or her future inner child) feels respected, cared for, and loved.

The good news is that as adults, if our inner child is wounded, we can rewrite that script. We can nurture, console, comfort, encourage, and psychologically hug our inner child to let him or her know that we are there for them in ways that are loving, forgiving, and accepting.

GRACEFUL GOODBYES IN REAL LIFE

PUT SOMETHING GOOD IN EVERY GOODBYE: Every LIFE CLUE we've talked about in this book goes back to this piece of advice: *See the bigness in the little.* What is true for children is true for all of us. When we turn our full attention to the little ones in our lives, we see clearly that their truths are our truths. Many of the things our adult minds are telling us are complicated really aren't.

Take saying goodbye. Preschoolers respond well when they know what to expect, right? Same for everyone no matter what the age. We would do well to acknowledge the primal importance of saying proper goodbyes. Saying goodbye is like giving your child and your inner child a lovely interval to prepare for the change that is about to happen.

Saying goodbye is never a small or insignificant gesture. The purpose is to deliver the kindness, courtesy, and respect that everyone deserves. In the Caribbean, people say, "I go to come back," which to me is a beautiful way to define a goodbye.

GRATEFUL FOR ALL THE GOODBYES:

If you think about it, saying goodbye is good because it means that we said hello and spent time with someone. Being grateful for the time we spend together is another small act of kindness that goes a long way toward happiness. So **embrace** so longs.

We live in a "more is more" reality. When we find something we love, we want more of it. We want more time, we crave more money, we want more things, we want more and more of life. Logically, we know that it's not the quantity but the quality of life that matters. More time isn't always the answer. Happiness is nurtured by being more grateful for the time that was shared.

SOMETIMES LESS IS MORE:

For preschoolers, sometimes their favorite toy is the box that the toy came in. Sometimes preschoolers are happy to sit on the floor and bang pots and pans with a wooden spoon. The ordinary is extraordinary. Simple is sometimes elegant. And nothing is simpler and more elegant than honoring the time we have together. Saying goodbye underscores that we are grateful for what we shared together. We can say thank you for the time we had together, and we can go one step further and make plans to see each other again. This is nourishment. Furthermore, as an adult, we can continue to nourish and do the work to heal our inner child.

**LIFE
CLUE
#20**

Put It All Together

Dear Reader,

I began this book with a note to you and I will bring this book to a close in the same way.

During my junior year in college, I was a teacher's assistant in a campus preschool, and I was having a hard time finding my way. One time I started to pass out the lunches too early, before we sang our "It's Time for Lunch" song. Exasperated, I slumped down next to the kids, tried to smile, and joined in the singing of the cute little lunch song. Then suddenly, I felt the softest squeeze of my hand. I looked down. Caroline, the smallest girl in the class, leaned over and whispered in my ear. She said, "Don't worry, Angela, you'll get it—and I know you'll be a great teacher." She smiled at me encouragingly, continued singing, and didn't let go of my hand. My heart melted with gratitude for little Caroline. I realized how smart children are, how intuitive, and how much love and empathy they have to give. I started to suspect then what I know now: If we follow their lead, we will be more joyous, more in alignment with ourselves, and more successful. As I said earlier, if we pay attention to children's ways—the small as well as the big things they do—we can change not only ourselves but also the world.

Let's continue to embrace life's lessons and follow the clues. One of the many things that the children in our lives remind us of is that they Like You Just the Way You Are (LIFE CLUE #1). They don't care what you look like or even what you bring them. They just want to be with you. We need to love ourselves as we are and surround ourselves with people who give us unconditional support and love. It makes life that much sweeter.

During your next conversation, lean in to the power we gain when we Take a Moment (LIFE CLUE #2), observe body language, and ask follow-up questions as we listen attentively and see what power can be found in that little moment of space.

May you always look up and into the universe to Find Your Clues (LIFE CLUE #3). You will be surprised that so many clues exist around you that will lead you toward happiness. Have you bumped into the same person three times? That's a clue. Have you accidentally dialed an old friend? That's a clue. Follow those clues and see where they take you.

Think about how much fun children have with the simple games they play every day. Then think about how you, as an adult, never seem to have time for anything, let alone play. Remember these ideas and Never Stop Playing (LIFE CLUE #4). Play in little ways—skip a rock over the lake, jump in a puddle, guess how many steps it takes to get to work, wear colorful socks, or paint your toenails red. Keep things light to bring more play and joy into **your life**.

When something seems bad, Always Try to Find Something Good (LIFE CLUE #5). Take it from Daniel Tiger: You can find a silver lining in most situations. Sometimes the "something good" is that you get to be with your family for comfort, or have time to rest. Sometimes the "something good" is that you can forget about having the "perfect party" and just have a party. Remember, smushed cake tastes good, too!

When you have to make a decision, think it through; Use Your Mind (LIFE CLUE #6), and Take It One Step at a Time (LIFE CLUE #7). These two clues are a philosophy in and of themselves that will help us make hard decisions, overcome obstacles, and create a plan to tackle our problems. Not as easy as it sounds, but these two steps bring us to the idea that You Can Do Anything You Wanna Do (LIFE CLUE #8). You may not be able to be an Olympic swimmer, but you owe it to yourself to get in the pool and swim. If you do, you are one step closer to what you want, and you will experience joy in the act of trying to get there.

Take a page out of a preschooler's book and Cultivate Routines (LIFE CLUE #9). Take a walk outside; notice the leaves budding on the trees during springtime, perhaps stop to smell the flowers, and maybe even take your shoes off and run in the grass. Take a minute to breathe deeply and give yourself a little pep in your step the way you did when you were little. It very well may bring some newfound joy in your day.

The idea of a skidoo (LIFE CLUE #10) was one of those out-of-the blue moments that made sense when we were creating Blue's Clues. But, of course, it's a metaphor for life. Find something you are interested in and immerse yourself in it. Read books on it. Go to the park, beach, or mountain and drink in the atmosphere. Actively going out and skidooing is one of the best ways to create a lasting memory for yourself and others.

Take a moment to make sure you Imagine, Every Day (LIFE CLUE #11), dream, and get lost in your thoughts. When you can imagine your future, you are much more likely to get it.

As great as it is to get out in the world and skidoo, it's also important to lie on the grass, look up at the stars, and Do Nothing, Together (LIFE CLUE #12). Have you ever lain on the grass with your head on a little one's belly and vice versa? The laughter that ensues will brighten anyone's day, which is another important clue: Laugh, Every Day (LIFE CLUE #13). There is science supporting how good laughter is for your overall health. No matter how serious life is, remember to find a moment to laugh, even if only to diffuse the situation with humor.

Take note that wherever you are, you can Create Your Own Neighborhood (LIFE CLUE #14). Like Daniel Tiger, be an active participant in your neighborhood and in the life you want to live. Do you want to live in a place where everyone knows your name? Start by saying hello to your neighbors. Do you want to bring people together for Halloween? Be the house or apartment that gives out fun treats to kids. Whatever it is, the more you give, the more you receive—it's a kindness loop.

Friends are the "magic beans" in life, so you would do well to Be Like Daniel Tiger and Buddy Up (LIFE CLUE #15). They can be friends from work, from the neighborhood, from high school or college, or the person you met on the train who makes the commute more enjoyable. Whoever they are, hold on to them and value the positivity they bring to your life.

Making our life richer starts with the love that you share with your spouse, children, and friends. If you feel it, say Ugga Mugga (LIFE CLUE #16). Don't wait until it's too late to let people know how much you love them.

There's an old expression, "the proof is in the pudding," so Don't Say Fun—Be Fun (LIFE CLUE #17). In every aspect of our lives we should focus on how the things we do demonstrate how much we care for our loved ones. Let others be the judge of what is fun—you just bring it!

And in order to bring it, you must Be Present (LIFE CLUE #18). When we are present and living in the moment, we will find more joy, laughter, and love. The rest can wait until later.

Honor the time you have with someone and Always Say Goodbye (LIFE CLUE #19). You don't have to sing a closing song (although I bet kids of all ages in your life would love it if you did!), but look that person in the eye and acknowledge the importance of your shared moment. And then lastly, Put It All Together (LIFE CLUE #20), and take a step in a new and awesome direction.

Thank you wholeheartedly for sharing this precious time with me. As our journey together comes to a close, I want to encourage you to seek and discover your own LIFE CLUES. Each day presents a new opportunity to unlock hidden treasures, unravel profound insights, and uncover the magic that lies inside us and outside, all around. Embrace the wonders that await you, for life's greatest mysteries often are concealed in the simplest moments.

Starting now, may you embark on a remarkable quest to find your own life clues that will lead you to rewarding relationships, fulfillment, and joy. Farewell for now. May our paths cross again in this extraordinary adventure we call *life*.

With Love,
Angela

About the Author

Angela C. Santomero is the co-creator of the award-winning *Blue's Clues* franchise. She is also the creator of the Emmy Award-winning *Daniel Tiger's Neighborhood* as well as the hit show *Super Why!*

A protégé of Fred Rogers, Angela has devoted her life to empowering kids and parents while also making them laugh. She lives in New York City with her husband and two daughters.